Last Man Out

Last Man Out

Glenn McDole, USMC,
Survivor of the Palawan Massacre
in World War II

BOB WILBANKS

McFarland & Company, Inc., Publishers
Jefferson, North Carolina, and London

Library of Congress Cataloguing-in-Publication Data

Wilbanks, Bob, 1931–
    Last man out : Glenn McDole, USMC, survivor of the
Palawan massacre in World War II / Bob Wilbanks.
        p.   cm.
    Includes bibliographical references and index.

    ISBN 0-7864-1822-2 (softcover : 50# alkaline paper)

    1. McDole, Glenn.   2. Palawan Barracks (Concentration
camp).   3. World War, 1939–1945—Prisoners and
prisons, Japanese.   4. Palawan Massacre, Philippines, 1944.
5. Prisoners of war—United States—Biography.
6. Prisoners of war—Philippines—Biography.   I. Title.
D805.5.P35W55   2004
940.54'7252'092—dc22   2004018233

British Library cataloguing data are available

Cover photograph: remants of *B shelter* inside the Palawan camp
with the charred bones and ashes of prisoners (U.S. War Department)

Manufactured in the United States of America

McFarland & Company, Inc., Publishers
  Box 611, Jefferson, North Carolina 28640
    www.mcfarlandpub.com

To the 139 American prisoners of war who
were slaughtered by soldiers of the Japanese Imperial
Army on December 14, 1944, at the Puerto Princea
Prison Camp, Palawan Island, in the Phillippines.

Acknowledgments

This book would not have been possible had it not been for Kathy McDole, Glenn McDole's daughter. She gathered old War Department files and put on paper Glenn's account of what happened to him and his buddies, who fought on Corregidor in 1942 and later ended up prisoners of war on Palawan Island, the Philippines. For Kathy McDole, it was a labor of love for a man who is now one of the few living survivors of what became known as the Palawan Massacre.

Putting this book together has not been easy; after all, the events in this story took place over 60 years ago, and the memories of the few still living who experienced it are beginning to fade.

I am deeply indebted to Jack Shelley, a longtime Iowa broadcast journalist with WHO Radio and Television, and retired professor of journalism at Iowa State University; Don Muhm, retired farm editor of *The Des Moines Register*; Don's wife, Joann; Bekki Rannebarger; Glenn McDole; and my wife, Jane.

Shelley, who was a war correspondent in Europe and the Pacific during the Second World War, continually asked questions with the merciless zest of a professor who had corrected student papers for 20 years—which he had.

Don Muhm, who also wore khaki, but served during the Korean War, was the first to tell me I had a manuscript that was worthy of a publisher's attention. He read it, critiqued it, made suggestions on form and content, and encouraged me to keep at it.

Joann Muhm was my cheerleader. When I had my doubts, she, along with my wife, Jane, gave me the confidence I needed.

Thanks are also due to Bekki Rannebarger, a whiz-kid at the computer who kept me on track.

My sincere gratitude goes to former Marine Glenn McDole: I thank him for his patience while I pried into his past for hours on end.

I offer my sincere thanks to all of these people.

Table of Contents

Preface

In the great Pacific War, 40 percent of American and Allied POWs died from starvation, torture, execution and disease in Japanese prison camps. Almost all the prisoners were slave laborers. Those too weak to work received only half the food of their comrades, who barely survived on a single mess kit of bug- and worm-infested rice per day. They worked from dawn to dusk, six to seven days a week.

At the outset of World War II, Japan's armies had captured thousands of American and Allied soldiers, sailors and Marines, and there is little doubt among historians that all of them would have been executed had Japan won the war. But the armada sweeping toward Japan across the Pacific, and two huge bombs, one which fell on Hiroshima and the other on Nagasaki, ended all thoughts of killing the thousands of prisoners scattered across Asia and the Pacific.

The Japanese war machine required labor, and a lot of it. The demand for the raw materials to make guns and other weapons for its war of conquest in the Pacific and Asia was more than its citizenry could provide, so it used slave labor.

The book you are about to read is the story of one of the Palawan survivors, Glenn McDole, of Ankeny, Iowa. In 1940, McDole was a hot-tempered, good-looking 19-year-old Urbandale, Iowa, high school dropout. Angry because he would be too old to play basketball his senior year, he stormed out of school. He thought about his future and decided to join the U.S. Marine Corps until he became old enough to enter the Iowa Highway Patrol. He joined the very next day and, soon after, headed off to boot camp in San Diego, California.

1

After boot camp, Mac, as his buddies called him, was shipped to the Philippines. It was peacetime, and those in the enlisted ranks didn't think or talk much about the rumors of war in the Pacific. It was good duty in the Philippines, and Mac's only regret was that he had not been shipped to Shanghai, China, where he would have been stationed with the famed China Marines, the 4th Marine Regiment. When the China Marines were shipped out of China to the Philippines, Mac finally got his wish. His battalion became part of the famed regiment shortly after all hell broke loose in the Pacific on December 7, 1941.

Mac fought on Corregidor until it was surrendered to the Japanese on May 6, 1942, and for nearly two and a-half years, he and his buddies were subjected to hard labor, repeated beatings, near-fatal illnesses, torture and near starvation. He was given just enough food to keep him alive for work as a slave laborer.

This is a story of survival. It is McDole's story of what happened to him and his comrades as they shared food and cared for each other with a grim determination to survive. You'll find a cross section of American youth in this story, young men from across the United States who were the children of the Great Depression and were toughened by it. Then came the slaughter and the mad scramble to stay alive. This book takes you through all of it: the fighting on Corregidor, Glenn McDole's capture and imprisonment by the Japanese, the brutal beatings and executions, surviving in conditions no Iowa farmer would impose on his cattle or hogs, and that terrible day when 139 young Americans were slaughtered.

Lady Luck must have been looking over the shoulders of the eleven young men who survived the slaughter as they made their way to freedom by swimming the bay and then walking to safety through the jungle of Palawan. There is nothing pretty about this story—no rose gardens or love letters from home—as you follow a young, scarred Glenn McDole, who found himself to be the last man out of Puerto Princesa, Palawan Prison Camp 10A.

This terrible event occurred over 60 years ago, and we have done our best to keep all the events in this book as accurate as possible. Although memories dim over time, both Glenn and I have gone over the timeline of events in this book many times, and we're both satisfied with the story you are about to read.

It should be noted that a little over a month after the Palawan Massacre, 123 hand-picked members of the U.S. Army 6th Rangers Battalion slipped through enemy lines on the island of Luzon, killed all the Japanese guards, and rescued over 500 sick and dying prisoners at the Cabanatuan prison camp. This successful life-saving mission was told in the best seller *Ghost Soldiers*, by Hampton Sides. The daring rescue was brought about, in part, because of the slaughter of the 139 American POWs on Palawan. Later, there were other rescue operations in the Philippines, including an airborne drop behind Japanese lines which saved the lives of American and British men, women and children in a civilian prison camp.

And now, here is Glenn (Mac) McDole's story.

Prologue

Had he been duck hunting, it would have been an easy left-to-right shot, but he wasn't firing at a mallard. His target was a Jap Zero, flying low toward the east over Manila Bay, not more than 150 yards from the end of his rifle barrel. A good shot, had it been stationary, but it was moving fast, and Sergeant Squeaky Myrick, firing his .50-caliber water-cooled machine gun at the same target, yelled, "Shoot him between the eyes, Mac!" The young Marine gave his target plenty of lead and fired a round from his .30-caliber Springfield. There was no indication he'd hit the Zero; it banked just enough to the right so he could see the pilot thumb his nose.

Corporal Glenn McDole, called Mac by his buddies, watched as the Zero moved quickly out of range of Ft. Hughes's antiaircraft guns and then took a hard right for another pass over Corregidor. There weren't many targets left on the bomb-scarred island fortress, and it would fall into Japanese hands in a week or so, bringing about the enslavement of thousands of U.S. and Filipino servicemen. It would be a long, long walk through Hell for all of them, including Corporal McDole.

1

Pearl Harbor

Monday, December 8, 1941

A gentle breeze off Manila Bay helped cool the huge, two-story, L-shaped barracks at the U.S. Navy Yard at Cavite in the Philippines. It was a little after 3:30 a.m., and the men of the 1st Separate Marine Battalion, those who weren't on guard duty, were asleep. The day before had been a typical workday: guard duty, front-gate security at the naval base, gunnery practice and all the other tasks required of a peacetime Marine Corps.

The early morning quiet was shattered by the piercing sound of the battalion bugler's call to arms. Lights went on throughout the barracks, and the men, all in their skivvies, dressed hurriedly and ran to formation in front of the barracks. Private First Class Glenn McDole sat bolt upright when he heard the call to arms. A Marine from Urbandale, Iowa, and a member of "M" Company, he wondered what was going on as he ran outside and lined up with his buddies in the predawn. They moved fast; it took only about five minutes for the men to dress and line up in formation. It wasn't often a Marine heard the bugler's call to arms, and that call, above all others, meant trouble. In the months and years ahead, there wasn't a man in the battalion who would forget the sound of the bugle that morning and the first few minutes of what was to become a long and savage war.

Lieutenant Colonel John P. Adams was the battalion's commanding officer. As he stepped in front of the formation, you could tell he wasn't the John Wayne type. His physique and demeanor didn't command a lot of attention, but most of the men thought of him as a good leader and a fair man in his day-to-day dealings with the battalion, and he was not one

5

given to long-winded oratory. Called to attention, then put at ease, Lieutenant Colonel Adams wasted no time informing his men about the rarely heard bugle alert: "The Japanese have bombed Pearl Harbor and we are at war. From now on you are to stand by your guns at all times." That was it. Adams called them to attention once again and then dismissed them. Although it was Monday, December 8, in the Philippines, it was Sunday, December 7, on the other side of the international dateline, and the war was coming their way. Stunned by what they'd just heard, the young Marines broke ranks and ran to the barracks to get their rifles and helmets and then head to their posts. Less than an hour before Adams' announcement, Japanese bombers had all but destroyed America's Pacific Fleet at Pearl Harbor and word of the sneak attack spread quickly to all U.S. ships and bases in the Pacific. By the time the young Marines of Cavite Navy Yard ran to the barracks, Japanese bombers had finished their work at Pearl and were flying back to their carriers.

Glenn McDole could hardly believe what he'd just heard and, as he ran into the barracks, he yelled to his buddy, Rufus Smith, a lean, tall Texan, "I can't believe it, Smitty. I can't believe the Japs could attack so close to the U.S.!" His voice quivering, Smitty looked at his Iowa buddy and said, "I wonder what's going to happen now, Mac?" There was no answer as the two men entered the barracks, grabbed their rifles and helmets and made a mad dash for their posts. The two men had been close friends since Mac's assignment to the naval yard in February of 1940, and both of them were well-trained Marines. Smitty ran to the base's ammunition dump, which he helped guard, and Mac headed to his post as an antiaircraft machine gunner.

There was a lot of confusion that morning. With an aerial attack a real possibility at any time, orders were changed. The Navy was concerned about the safety of six PBY bombers located in Manila Harbor, so they flew them to Los Baños, at that time a small resort city on the Laguna de Bay about 50 miles east of Manila. Los Baños ("The Baths") derived its name from the thermal springs that flowed from the base of Mount Makiling. The waters were piped into the town's hotels. Mac would not have the luxury of the baths while he was in Los Baños. Somebody had to guard and camouflage the bombers, and McDole was one of twelve Marines picked that day to provide security for the planes. In all that confusion, he went looking for Smitty and his other buddy, Roy Henderson, hoping they could volunteer for the Los Baños duty. The three of them were inseparable, all starters on the battalion basketball team, they went everywhere together. The team had a winning record playing other service teams in the Philippines, but on December 8, Pearl Harbor Day, there were no more thoughts of basketball or the good times spent on liberty in Cavite and

Manila. McDole looked everywhere for his buddies, but with time running out, he jumped aboard a Navy truck with eleven other enlisted men and took off for Los Baños. Second Lieutenant William Hogaboom, a recent Annapolis graduate from Vicksburg, Mississippi, was in charge of the squad. He was younger than those he commanded and the enlisted men called him "Chick"—short for "chicken." But, of course, they didn't call him that when he was within earshot.

It was a typically hot, humid and sunny day as the truck carrying the Marines rolled into Los Baños and then to the beach where the six PBY flying boats were floating just offshore. When they jumped from the back of the truck, Mac got his first real taste of living and surviving in the Philippine jungle. He would get to know it even better in the months ahead. When he stepped into the forest, he was awed by its darkness—sunlight couldn't penetrate the overhead layered foliage—and the screeches and howls coming from monkeys, birds and other exotic wildlife seemed almost deafening. Mac had come to this place from the open, rolling hills and flat fields of Iowa, and it would take him awhile to get used to the new environment.

While it was peaceful in Los Baños that December afternoon, Japanese bombers and fighters were in the process of wiping out half the bomber force and a third of the fighter planes elsewhere in the Philippines, hitting Clark Field where the B-17s were neatly arranged along the runway awaiting refueling while their crews ate lunch.

When he walked to the beach and saw the half-dozen bombers, Mac looked at Lieutenant Hogaboom and innocently asked, "How are we going to get these planes out of the water and into the jungle?" Hogaboom just looked at McDole and smiled. A short time later the 185-pound, 5'10", McDole and eleven other Marines waded into the water and pulled the planes, one-by-one, onto the beach, through the sand and into the jungle. They did everything they could to camouflage and conceal them. They cut down trees to clear a spot for them and then covered the planes with foliage and palm leaves. The camouflage looked real good, and for two days the squad stood guard over the bombers.

On the second day, they heard the strange roar of engines and a sound not at all like a PBY or B-17 would make. They looked out over the water and saw them coming—Japanese bombers, flying in low, right toward the shoreline and aimed right at them. Mac and the others scattered deeper into the jungle. They knew there was nothing they could do. They looked on helplessly as all six PBYs were blown to pieces. For Glenn McDole, it was his first experience as a target for Japanese bombardiers, but he would be targeted again. Watching his bombers go up in flames was frustrating because he was unable to fight back. Adding to his frustration was word that the naval yard at Cavite had been bombed—obliterated shortly after they left the base. Their two-story barracks no longer existed.

While the Marine squad waited for their next assignment, Philippine and American forces were rounding up all Japanese citizens in the Philippines and taking them to Manila for interrogation. All of them knew now that a Japanese invasion was imminent. There were scattered reports of sabotage, and several Japanese citizens had been taken into custody in Los Baños. Mac and the rest of his squad searched a small Japanese-owned hotel, whose owner had been taken into custody by Filipino soldiers. After a thorough search of the building, they found evidence of espionage—photos of the six camouflaged PBYs they had hidden in the jungle.

The Invasion

Mac's squad was still on duty at Los Baños, December 22, when the Japanese invaded the Philippines. He learned later that 72 Japanese transports, escorted by battleships and cruisers and carrying General Masaharu Homma's 14th Army, had poured ashore on three beachheads in the Lingayen Gulf. A few hours later, a smaller task force put troops ashore at Davao on the southern island of Mindanao. General MacArthur was right when he predicted the Japanese would land on those beaches, but he was dead wrong as to the timing and outcome. He'd predicted an April, 1942, attack, when Japanese troops, he said, would be stopped on the beaches. It didn't work out that way. The half-trained Philippine Army, which outnumbered Japanese forces by two-to-one, was no match. The Japanese moved quickly across the countryside. MacArthur had no choice other than to implement *Plan Orange*, a well-rehearsed retreat to the Bataan Peninsula. He did so on December 23, after learning that additional Japanese troops had landed 60 miles southeast of Manila. The fate of thousands of Filipino and American soldiers, sailors and Marines had been sealed, and Glenn McDole, the young man from Urbandale, Iowa, was among them.

Christmas Eve, McDole and the rest of the squad received orders to go to Manila and report in at the YMCA. Although Mac didn't know exactly what his next assignment would be, he looked forward to Manila. He was happy to leave what had become a boring watch in Los Baños and, besides, he hadn't had a decent shower in two weeks, having spent most of his time living in the jungle and then sleeping in old, dilapidated, abandoned Philippine militia barracks.

Christmas in Manila

After the 50-mile ride from Los Baños on Christmas Day, 1941, Mac jumped off the truck in front of the Manila YMCA. As he walked to the building, he heard someone yell, "Where in hell you been, Mac?" He turned to see "Red Rider," a Chaplain from the Cavite Navy Yard. The Marines had given the chaplain that nickname because of the big red beard he'd grown. "My God, Mac, we thought you'd been killed in the Navy yard bombings! You'd better get word home to your family because I'm sure they sent your mother a message telling her that you 'got it.'" Mac didn't waste any time. He ran to the telegraph office where he sent one of the last radiograms from Manila to his family in Iowa. All he could think

Glenn McDole sent this picture, taken in the Philippines before the war, to his mother, Dessa, in Urbandale.

was that his mother, Dessa, and his dad, David, must be worried sick. Back home, it was the day after Christmas, and it was welcome news for the McDole family. It was the best gift they had ever received.

As he walked back to the Y, Mac thought about his home and his family. They were a close-knit clan, drawn together by the hard times of the Great Depression. His father, also nicknamed "Mac," was a sign painter by trade and handy enough to take on any number of other jobs to support his wife, Dessa, and their six children: Max, the oldest; then Glenn; the youngest brother, little Joe; and sisters Colleen, Dolores and Margaret.

During the depression, the family had many addresses, always moving to wherever the elder McDole could find work. He and his wife were Nebraskans, and as their family had grown they moved to California, then to Colorado, and back to Nebraska, where the elder McDole homesteaded some land at the western edge of the state. Then it was off to Overton, Texas, where Glenn was born. In 1936 the family moved to Urbandale, Iowa. They decided to make it their last stop and settled into a house at 70th and Douglas streets.

Glenn's mother, Dessa, was a little woman, 4'10", with fiery red hair. She held the family together while her husband worked at various jobs in Iowa and surrounding states. Since David McDole went anywhere there was work to be had, he was away from his family for long periods, but when he was home, he and young Mac spent time fishing and hunting together. At times, when there was no work to be had, Mac and his dad would spend up to a week hunting and chasing game with their two coon dogs. The elder McDole had taught his son how to work the dogs, and they had great times in the field. The two Macs were very close, and David McDole instilled in his son the love for hunting, fishing and the outdoors, where, in later years, he would spend a lot of time.

The day after Christmas, 1941, General MacArthur declared Manila an "open city," which, in Geneva Convention parlance, meant that neither U.S., nor Filipino, forces would contest Japanese occupation of the city. The hope was that the city would not be a target for bombs after U.S. and Filipino forces had been evacuated. All U.S. and Filipino forces were moving out of Manila and executing a strategic withdrawal to Bataan, where it was hoped the Japanese could be stopped, or at least delayed until help arrived. But there was a growing awareness among the American soldiers, sailors and Marines that there would be no U.S. rescue operation in the Philippines. Still, many of the American and Filipino GIs manning the gun emplacements looked wistfully out to sea hoping to see the outline of an American armada coming to their rescue.

To Corregidor

On the day when MacArthur declared Manila an open city, Private First Class Glenn McDole was ordered to Corregidor to join other members of the 1st Separate Marine Battalion. As he stepped aboard the motor launch with about thirty other men for the short water trip to what they called "The Rock," he remembered his first trip there. He'd spent a month on Corregidor shortly after arriving in the Philippines on the 14th day of February, 1941, where he was a guard at the Naval Radio Intercept Station.

Mac and the other enlisted Marines didn't realize all that was really happening in the Pacific, but their cockiness prevailed and they formed their own conclusions about the war. To him and his buddies at foxhole level, it was only a matter of time before they'd beat the hell out of the Japs. There were no thoughts about losing battles, being wounded or killed, or becoming prisoners of war. Such things never entered their minds, but when he stepped off the launch at Bottomside on Corregidor, Mac left behind a Navy Yard destroyed by Japanese bombers and the city of Manila wide open to the Japanese. By the time Japanese bombs started falling on Manila, nearly 17,000 Navy, Marine Corps, Army and Filipino servicemen were crammed into Corregidor's network of tunnels and fortifications. Unfortunately, most of them were not front-line troops, but in the final fateful days of the siege many of them—sailors and soldiers who knew little about shooting a gun—became front-line fighters.

Mac's "home" for the next few months wasn't much to look at. Located at the entrance to Manila Bay, Corregidor divided the bay into two channels: to the north, looking toward the Bataan Peninsula, a very narrow channel about three miles wide; and to the south a much wider expanse of water, maybe six miles wide, looking toward Cavite and the bombed out U.S. navy yard.

If you look at Corregidor from above, it looks like a tadpole with its tail swinging to the left. It's almost four miles long from east to west and has an average width of a mile. The tail was called "Bottomside" and had two docking facilities and the only beaches where troop landings could occur. At the base of the tail was Malinta Hill, high and formidable. "Middleside" was west of the hill, where schools, officers' quarters and other

An aerial view of Corregidor. The tail of the tadpole-shaped island, where Japanese troops made their landing, is in the foreground (U.S. War Department).

facilities were located. The highest point was "Topside," which had a two-story stone barracks, one of the biggest in the world at that time. Some considered it almost bombproof. Most of the big sea-defense gun batteries were located on Topside. In all, there were 23 big gun batteries on Corregidor, from huge 14-inch cannons to 10-inch mortars, and all dating from before the Air Age and designed to protect the anchorages of Manila Bay from enemy ships.

Mac was seldom inside Corregidor's famed tunnel complex, which was hailed as an engineering marvel when it was formed in 1932. The complex, drilled through solid rock on Malinta Hill, was 1,400-feet long and had 25 lateral tunnels, each 150 yards long, branching out on either side. The huge bomb shelter contained a complete hospital, ammunition storage, communications, offices and motor fuel storage. In the final days of the battle for the Philippines, it would be a haven for the wounded and the nerve center for officers and men making their final stand against the Japanese.

December 27, 1941

Mac's first job on Corregidor was as a security guard at MacArthur's headquarters. He was on duty outside the general's office the day the Japanese ignored MacArthur's open city declaration and bombed Manila. A colonel walked into MacArthur's office and said, "General, I've just received information that the Japs have bombed Manila, and they hit a parochial school!" Mac watched as MacArthur half rose from his chair behind a giant teakwood desk and said, "Those goddamn Japs! They did what?" He told the colonel to get a radio message to his Japanese contact in Manila and tell him, "If they bomb Manila once more, I'll make Tokyo look like mud and sand!" He finished his order by slamming his fist down on the desk. Mac couldn't help but smile, and he whispered to himself, "Go get 'em, General!" At this point, MacArthur had not talked to any of the enlisted men who stood guard at his command post, including Mac, but they would meet later.

Two days later, the young Marine watched from his bomb shelter as eighteen Japanese Navy bombers attacked Corregidor, dropping their first payload and starting the air war over the island. It was a typically hot day as the bombs came whistling down on the headquarters and barracks at "Middleside." There were many casualties among those who were still asleep on the second floor of the barracks. Mac watched it all from his hole in the ground, and an hour later Japanese planes returned to drop even more bombs. The second raid wasn't as successful. They all cheered as four Japanese bombers fell from the sky. It was a minor victory for Corregidor's antiaircraft gunners.

MacArthur didn't like the tunnel offices on Topside, and elected instead to set up shop on Middleside. This meant there would be no barracks for Mac, and with the number of men now on the island, it was a case of sleeping wherever there was space for a shelter half and a blanket. Although the days were long and hot, it was the dry season, and he didn't miss the mosquitoes, which had engulfed him on the mainland. His work days were long, a good night's sleep was rare and, when on duty, he could sense the growing tension and anxiety among the officers and men as they entered MacArthur's headquarters.

It was sundown, and Mac was standing guard outside the main entrance to MacArthur's headquarters. He looked up to see a solitary figure walk out the entrance and stop in front of him. He was tall, wore a crumpled hat and, as he looked Mac over carefully, he pulled a pipe from his mouth and asked, "What's your name, soldier?" This was quite a moment for the young Midwesterner. He snapped to attention and saluted MacArthur. He gave his name and rank, and the general told Mac to stand down, have a seat and relax. Both of them sat down and started talking. The general asked about Mac's family, and Mac told him about his life as a civilian and his family back in Iowa. It felt good to talk to someone, and this man seemed to really care about him. They were having a pleasant, relaxing conversation when a sergeant of the guard walked up and began berating Mac for sitting down in the presence of the general. He told him it was a court-martial offense. MacArthur looked at the sergeant and told him that he'd ordered Mac to sit down, then told him to mind his own business. Although the general had friends, and lots of enemies, he made a friend that night. MacArthur was an "all-right guy" as far as Mac was concerned, no matter what his critics said of him.

Japanese bombers kept pounding the island fortress every day. One of Mac's most frustrating duties was escorting MacArthur to his bomb shelter when the air raid sirens sounded. The Rock's antiquated radar system didn't give them much warning time, so when the sirens blared out across the island, everybody ran to the shelters. MacArthur never did. He strolled to the shelter, looking skyward and talking about what the Japs might have planned for them. The General's leisurely strolls nearly drove Mac nuts. Of course, a PFC couldn't tell a General to speed it up, and about all he could do was casually point out: "The bombs should be falling any second, General."

When McDole's 1st Separate Marine Battalion moved to Corregidor, it became the 3rd Battalion, 4th Marine Regiment. The famed 4th Marines, or "China Marines," had been stationed in Shanghai for 15 years, protecting American interests there. With war on the horizon, the China Marines, a tough, well-trained and disciplined outfit, slipped out of Shanghai without incident and were ordered to the Philippines, where they arrived shortly before the war erupted. Before Admiral Thomas Hart moved his command out of the Philippines, as the Japanese were closing in on Manila, he turned over command of the 4th Marines to General MacArthur. The China Leathernecks chafed at the thought of being commanded by an Army General, even though it was Douglas MacArthur. When the general ordered the 4th Marines to Corregidor to man the beach defenses, some critics claimed the China Marines would be nothing more than the general's personal guard. Glenn McDole couldn't have been happier. He'd wanted to be a China Marine since boot camp. Now his battalion was part of the famed 4th Marine Regiment.

Mac had very little time off, but when he did, he'd walk around the island hoping to see familiar faces. He'd all but given up finding his buddies, Smitty and Henderson, thinking maybe they'd been early casualties of the Japanese bombs dropped on the Navy yard. No one he talked to had any idea where they might be. Meanwhile, the bombings increased. Not a day passed without at least one flight of bombers hitting the island, and two raids a day were becoming common. As the bombs fell, the landscape changed. The bombs destroyed all the foliage. The island fortress looked more like a scarred landscape pocked with bomb craters and littered with twisted steel and barb wire.

Duty on Ft. Hughes

Mac was doing the job well, and that merited some recognition. Colonel Adams promoted Mac to corporal and assigned him to Ft. Hughes, where he helped man a water-cooled .50-caliber machine gun. When called upon, he also helped load and fire the fort's big, 14-inch "disappearing" gun. The huge gun was located below ground level, was elevated to firing position by scissors-like hydraulics, and then lowered itself back when it was fired. The big guns were in huge emplacements on Corregidor, aimed at protecting the waterways north and south of the island. Mac's machine gun position was directly below the muzzle of the 14-inch gun, and he was warned to abandon his machine gun emplacement when the big one was fired. The blast was deafening, the concussion tremendous, as he found out one day when he fell asleep and the huge gun just above him was loaded and fired across the bay to the hills above Cavite, where the Japanese were moving artillery. The blast was so intense, and the concussion so massive, that he staggered out of the gun emplacement and waited for some time before his senses returned to normal. They forgot to warn him they were going to fire the big gun, but after that he never again fell asleep in his gun emplacement.

The small hunk of rock Mac defended was officially called Fort Hughes, but to the Filipinos it was Caballo Island, located less than a half-mile south of Corregidor. The island was about a half-mile long and a couple hundred yards wide and was heavily fortified with its big, 14-inch rifle and 10-inch mortars aimed toward Cavite, some six miles across the bay. Mac wasn't too impressed when he stepped off the motor launch onto the little island, where he'd be one of 250 men who would man the guns, but he had no problem fitting into the daily routine. He spent 24 hours a day on duty at his machine gun emplacement, and when the big artillery piece was to be fired, he was called on to help load the 440 pounds of powder it took to propel a 1,500-pound shell across Manila Bay to the Cavite shore. He slept when he could. Life settled down to a daily routine of air raids, hunkering down for a little sleep, and meals of powdered eggs and beans. Mac never said, "What's for chow?" He knew it would be eggs and beans twice a day, every day, for the duration.

As long as Corregidor's big guns and the guns on Ft. Hughes and Ft. Drum remained in working condition, there would be no Japanese ships in Manila Harbor. However, the only opposition to the Japanese bombers and fighters were the antiaircraft guns, and as the number of air raids increased and Japanese bombers found their targets, the number of antiaircraft emplacements began to shrink. Japanese pilots became bolder, and their low-level strafing missions became more numerous. As enemy forces moved even closer to the Bataan Peninsula, the big guns on Corregidor and Ft. Hughes were put to work. Soon Japanese artillery fire from Cavite, an area occupied by the Japanese since shortly after the first of the year, rained down on Ft. Hughes. On February 6, 1942, a day when Japanese artillery shells hit the fort with a vengeance, Mac celebrated his twenty-first birthday hunkered down in a bomb shelter. Ft. Hughes's gunners answered with 1,500-pound shells from the barrel of the 14-inch gun. Mac watched as the gun was fired and then recoiled, slowly lowering the barrel into the ground. Once reloaded, the huge gun's snout was raised from its bunker and fired again at the artillery positions in the hills overlooking Cavite. The fort's big mortars joined in during the daily shootouts. Spotters watched as Japanese guns were moved into position in the hills above Cavite, and then they put the big gun to work again, blowing away gun emplacements and causing havoc among Japanese gunners.

Mac stayed in his hole during the air raids and artillery fire throughout the morning. At noon, the guns were silent and remained so until about two in the afternoon. Ft. Hughes's defenders called this period their

"Japanese Siesta." But the rest period didn't last long. Shortly after 2 p.m., the enemy's artillery shells came screaming in again and kept it up throughout the day and into the night. The noon break in the bombardment gave Mac a chance to eat, walk down to water's edge, wash off the grime of battle and, if needed, get a haircut from the island's self-appointed barber. Shaving without a sharp blade, soap or warm water was too painful, so he let his beard grow while he was on Ft. Hughes. Later on, for sanitary reasons, he'd go beardless, finding a crude but effective way to shave without putting too many cuts and scrapes on his face by sharpening the steel insole of an old boot to near-razor sharpness.

March 11, 1942

It was quiet that night. Mac was in his gun emplacement looking out at the harbor. It was a dark night—there was no moon above, and Mac couldn't see beyond the shoreline. There had been a lull in the Japanese artillery and air raids. Off in the distance, he heard the low, guttural sound of powerful Marine engines in the harbor. They'd been told to expect friendly craft in the area at that time and to withhold their fire. It was dark and overcast and there was nothing to be seen on the water, just the sound of the engines moving at slow speed. Then, when the boats had cleared Corregidor and were in open water, the engines roared and the two boats picked up speed and moved quickly out to sea. The next day Mac learned it had been a pair of PT boats taking General MacArthur, his family and his staff to Mindanao, where they were to be flown to Australia. General Jonathon Wainwright was now in command of U.S. and Filipino forces in the Philippines.

The aerial bombings and artillery bombardments were relentless. Many days on Ft. Hughes, Mac could hardly see Corregidor, only a half mile across the water. With the dry season underway, smoke and dust from the constant bombardment blocked out any view of the rock, and the choking dust was an added irritant to the battered and weakened defenders. Considering the circumstances, though, Mac had no physical complaints. Even with little sleep and the stress of the constant bombardment as he huddled in a hole for protection, he hadn't lost much weight and seemed in fairly good shape. Although he hadn't found his two close buddies, Smitty and Henderson, he did have Sergeant Squeaky Myrick with him when he was sent to Ft. Hughes. Myrick was also a member of the Marine Navy Yard basketball team. Smitty and Myrick were "the wrecking crew"—the two members of the team who were called in when the score was close and the outcome of the game in doubt. Their job was to make life miserable for the opponents—an elbow here, an illegal block there and any other move that might save the game for the Marines. The team had a reputation of sorts, and towards the end of the season had trouble finding Navy teams to compete against them. Mac was a guard on the Marine team and had played high school basketball for Urbandale. His ineligibility for his senior year on the school's basketball team was the main reason he was now huddling in a hole while the Japanese were lobbing artillery shells and sending bombers and Zeros to bomb and strafe the fort, trying repeatedly to kill him and his buddies.

Looking Back

Oh, yes, there in the Philippines he remembered how he had ended up in the hellhole called Ft. Hughes. Urbandale had just finished the football season with a loss to Grimes, and Glenn was looking forward to the basketball season and the remainder of his senior year. He was older than most of his classmates. The depression years had kept the family on the move. Moving from state to state and school to school—and then not signing up for classes in Urbandale when they settled in Iowa—had set him back a year.

After the football game, Glenn was called in to Coach Don Perkins' office. He felt good. Although they'd lost the last game of the season, he was looking forward to playing basketball. Coach Perkins was a big man— 6'3", 200-pounds of meat and muscle. He had a way of inspiring confidence and providing the coaching skills that helped the young athletes win games. "Have a seat, Glenn," he mumbled, as Glenn walked into his office. Mac knew something was up when he called him "Glenn." He almost always used "Mac." The coach fumbled with his sleeves, rolling them up to the elbows, gave a deep sigh and said, "You're a tremendous athlete, Glenn, and you've been a great asset to this team and to this school." Mac sat there, a lump forming in his throat, and listened. "I've got some bad news for ya'. I just got done talking with the principal and he said...," Coach Perkins paused, then said, "Well, I guess you won't be able to play anymore sports this year. You're over the age limit, Glenn, and the rules say a 20-year-old can't play high school sports."

Glenn couldn't believe what the coach said. He was confused and sat there with his mouth open looking at Coach Perkins. Then he pleaded, "Coach, I've got the whole basketball season in front of me, what are you talking about?" His face flushed red, and he was angry. Coach looked at Mac and said, "I even tried talking to the principal to see if we could make an exception, but he said those were the age rules and he couldn't do any-

thing about it no matter how much he wanted to. Mac, I know he feels as
bad as I do! My God, Glenn, you're one of the best basketball players we've
got!" There was silence for a moment, then Mac stood and started for the
door. Coach Perkins made one last feeble attempt to soothe the hurt feelings and anger that consumed him. "Mac," he said, "why don't you continue coming to practice. You can help your team, maybe even become the
team manager." "Forget it!" Mac yelled, "I don't want to be an errand boy.
I want to play basketball." He stormed out of the office. As he walked away,
Mac realized the coach was sorry about the situation, but he still couldn't
help feeling angry and let down by what he thought were lousy rules lim-
iting competition because of age. Glenn would soon be twenty-years old,
and his playing days were over. Mac had a temper.

He didn't say anything when he walked out of the coach's office and
through the locker room. Although most of his teammates had congre-
gated there, not a word was said as he walked out of the room, slamming
the door shut on a couple of lockers as he walked out. That night Mac did
a lot of thinking, and looking back at what he should have done at the
time, he wished he'd never stayed out of school after the family had moved
to Urbandale from Texas. Then, he'd have been able to play his final year
of basketball. At that point in his life only two things mattered, sports and
family, and it was too late now to look back.

Mac went home. He didn't say anything when he walked in the door.
His family knew something was wrong, but no one said anything. They'd
let Mac tell his story when he felt like it. In early evening, some of his buddies came over to the house to offer their support. That helped relieve
some of the depression. They all hopped in Mac's Model A and spent the
rest of the evening at Reed's Ice Cream Parlor, a local high school hang-
out. Very few kids had a car in the late '30s, and under an agreement with
a man who owned a dairy, Mac had worked the whole summer delivering
milk without pay, with the understanding he'd have the Model A free and
clear at summer's end. Driving home that night, Mac had pretty well made
up his mind to quit school and find something to do until he was old
enough to join the highway patrol. He daydreamed about working as a
highway patrolman after talking to Mike Wilson, a well-known and
respected member of the Iowa Highway Patrol. Wilson often stopped to
watch the after-school football practice. In a seemingly offhand sugges-
tion, Wilson said, "Why don't you join the Marine Corps to fill in the time
before you're old enough to become a patrolman?" Wilson didn't bother
to tell Mac he was a former Marine.

Later that night Mac walked into the backyard and entered a trailer
home which took up most of the family's small backyard. The trailer once
was home to all of the McDole family as it moved about the west. Now, it

The rocky, barbed wire–strewn beach of Corregidor where Japanese troops faced stiff resistance by the American and Filipino soldiers, sailors and Marines (U.S. War Department).

had become Mac's bedroom. He slept alone in the trailer, a luxury in those days. Few young men living at home could say they had their own bedroom. It was a tight fit for the seven other McDoles living in the house at 70th and Douglas.

It was a fitful sleep for young Mac that night. Sometime after midnight, his eyes popped open and he sat up in bed. He knew now what he was going to do. When he got up in the morning, he dressed, had a pancake breakfast and headed to the federal building in downtown Des Moines. As he walked into the building, he passed the recruiting poster of Uncle Sam pointing his finger directly at Mac. "I Want You!" read the poster, and Mac didn't need any coaxing. He joined the United States Marine Corps. He would get his high school diploma later, while taking courses from the United States Armed Forces Institute at Cavite.

2

Surrender

Bataan Falls

On April 9, 1942, U.S. and Filipino forces on Bataan—battered, diseased and emaciated—surrendered to the Japanese. The next day, what became known as the Bataan Death March got underway under a blazing Philippine sun. Over 70,000 Allied POWs, including 12,000 Americans, were forced to make the 60-mile walk to Camp O'Donnell without food or water. Of the Americans, it is estimated that hundreds died from sickness, beatings, execution and other mistreatment at the hands of the Japanese. In one of the worst incidents of Japanese brutality, 300 Filipino scouts were lined up and executed by shooting, bayoneting and beheading. The Bataan defenders had fought bravely. But the Philippine Army had not been prepared, and it threw raw recruits and half-trained troops into the battle. American forces weren't much better off. The trained combat troops had fought side-by-side with sailors and army personnel who had little training in firing a rifle or machine gun or in throwing a hand grenade. By the time the the Bataan defenders reached Camp O'Donnell, only 54,000 remained. Some 7,000 to 10,000 died along the way. Some escaped into the jungle.

Of the allied soldiers on Bataan who tried to escape on the last day of the battle, only a handful made it across the narrow channel between the Bataan Peninsula to Corregidor. Many of those who tried to swim were blown out of the water by Japanese artillery, killed by riflemen or became food for sharks.

Now, the artillery duels began in earnest, and Corregidor, seen from Ft. Hughes when the dust and smoke cleared, would have looked like a

moonscape had it not been for the twisted steel and barbed wire. All vegetation on the once-lush island had been bombed or burned away. Hundreds of the wounded and sick jammed the passageways of the Malinta
Tunnel on Corregidor as the artillery and bombing raids increased at a
fiendish level.

It was no better on Ft. Hughes. Mac and his buddies could hear the
noises in the harbor, which indicated the Japanese were in the bay, en
force, and readying for a showdown. Gunners had fired so many shells
through the barrels of their huge 14-inch guns that the rifling in the barrels eroded and was worn away. In a frustrating attempt at downing the
Japanese bombers overhead, the island's 10-inch mortars were used as
antiaircraft weapons. Mac watched as gunners opened the mortar shells
and cut the fuses down to a bare minimum so they would explode in the
air, hopefully sending shrapnel into the bombers. Japanese dive bombers
tried every maneuver possible to skip or bounce their bombs into the
opening of the Malinta tunnel, where hundreds of wounded and battle-
weary troops had taken refuge. They soon discovered that they were easy
targets for the water-cooled .50s and, after losing a few aircraft, it was back
to a higher altitude.

Squeaky Myrick

Waves of planes hit the island in a continuous air bombardment. Mac
decided he needed a safer refuge and ran for a small foxhole. When he
jumped in he almost landed on Squeaky Myrick, and the two friends sat
with heads down and tried to talk of better times while the bombs and
artillery shells dropped around them.

"What happened to your buddy, Smith?" Squeaky asked. "I don't
have any idea where in hell Smitty went," Mac said. "No one has seen hide
nor hair of him or Roy Henderson since the Japs bombed the Navy Yard
at Cavite." Just as Mac had answered Squeaky, a bomb hit nearby. That
was all Squeaky could take. "Mac, it's gettin' too hot in here for me," he
yelled, "Let's get the hell outta' here!" "Damnit!" Mac yelled, "I'm not
about to stick my head out of this hole!" With shells falling all around
them, Squeaky panicked. Mac watched, dumbfounded, as Squeaky
jumped out of the gun emplacement and ran toward one of the bigger
emplacements about 15 yards away. It happened in a split second. Squeaky
jumped in just as a shell hit the emplacement dead center. Mac watched
in horror as Squeaky and the others in the shelter were blown to bits. With
body parts scattered over the area, Mac buried his head in his hands and
cried remembering Squeaky Myrick: a likable guy, a good sergeant and

a man who loved dancing, basketball, and the Corps. Mac had called him the "Jitterbug Man from Cavite" because of his talent for attracting young women to his dance hall table. Mac, Roy Henderson and Smitty had liked to go on liberty with Squeaky, because his dancing always attracted the ladies, and Mac could sit for hours nursing a rum and coke and talking to the young women who waited to dance with Squeaky. With shells bursting about him, Mac thought about his two drill instructors at boot camp in San Diego, who had declared they would separate the men from the boys. On that dirty, dusty, bomb-pocked, bloodstained island in Manila Harbor, Corporal Glenn McDole had survived still another close call and had kept his head about him. The drill instructors at the Marine Boot Camp had done their job, and Corporal McDole was doing his. His anger growing, he was unafraid and determined to fight to the end. The Marine Corps had done its best to prepare Mac and his buddies for what lay ahead. The training at San Diego boot camp was a constant, almost 24-hour-a-day program, to test the young men to the limit, both physically and psychologically. The training helped, but the pressure on the men who were surviving the intense day-after-day bombardment couldn't be duplicated in boot camp, and it was up to each man to keep his wits about him.

The situation on Corregidor and Ft. Hughes deteriorated rapidly. The shells kept raining down. The Army, Navy and Marines had given up any hope of American ships and planes coming to the rescue. All they could do was to delay the Japanese advance through the Pacific. Anticipating a landing almost anytime, Mac helped roll barrels of oil down to water's edge. Then, they fired at the barrels with their rifles and machine guns, sending a thick coat of oil over the coral. Mac took a look at the mess of black, slippery oil along the shoreline, the barbed wire and gun emplacements, and thought to himself that it would be all but impossible to make a successful landing. But the Japanese wouldn't be landing there.

The Iowa Marine had witnessed at least 300 air raids and the slow collapse of the island's defensive tools since the fall of Bataan. Communication facilities had been obliterated, telephone lines were cut by falling bombs faster than they could be repaired. Unless there was someone who would run from unit to unit with messages, there was no communication. However, there were a few who were brave enough to tempt Lady Luck by running the messages from one foxhole to another. With bombs and artillery falling constantly, the job was suicidal, but if one runner was killed or wounded, another man would volunteer, running like mad and spreading the word as he ran.

There is a great deal of bitterness when fighting a losing battle, and Bataan and Corregidor were no exception. Mac remembered many of the defenders of Bataan who felt their country had let them down, had failed to support them in their struggle to survive:

> *"We're the battling Bastards of Bataan*
> *No mama, no papa, no Uncle Sam;*
> *No aunts, no uncles, no cousins, no nieces*
> *No Pills, no planes, no artillery pieces;*
> *… and nobody gives a damn!"*

But that battle cry irritated Mac, he never took part in singing it with the other guys at Ft. Hughes. To the Iowa Marine, the United States was the most wonderful country in the world. He remembered what his dad told him: "Glenn, you only have one country and one family: don't ever give up on either of them for they'll always stand behind you, no matter what!" He didn't give up—the thought of surrender never entered his mind. He still believed the U.S. would return to rescue them. And he was strengthened even more knowing his family back in Iowa had not forgotten him. For their sake, he hoped they didn't know what was happening on Corregidor.

May 5, 1942

Someone yelled, "Here they come!" Looking out from his emplacement, Mac could see hundreds of Japanese boats heading towards Corregidor and Ft. Hughes. At least 2,000 Japanese troops tried hitting the beach in the first wave and American and Filipino gunners had a field day. The slaughter was horrendous. Rumor spread that the enemy casualty rate was about 70 percent, but there were still hundreds of landing craft in the bay waiting to disgorge more Japanese troops. Mac and his buddies on Ft. Hughes nearly managed to sweep the Japanese troops off the island; but by daybreak, the Japanese troops had gained a small foothold on the only beach area they could use—Corregidor's Bottomside.

While the Americans fought, General Wainwright was under increasing pressure from Japanese General Masaharu Homma to surrender unconditionally. With hundreds killed and hundreds more wounded and lying in the tunnels on Corregidor, Wainwright had no other choice: He surrendered all U.S. and Filipino forces on May 6, 1942.

A runner moved about Ft. Hughes telling Mac and the others what Wainwright had done. He told them to get rid of the ammunition, destroy the guns, stack the rifles and wait for further instructions. Mac and the GIs around him started crying at word of the surrender. He witnessed the deaths of two men, who yelled they were not about to surrender to "those Jap bastards" and then shot themselves. Still others tried to flee and some jumped into small boats and fled out to sea. Rumor had it that only one boat made it to safety.

Mac and the others left on Ft. Hughes took the bolts from their rifles and threw them into the bay. They drained the oil from the hydraulic systems of the big 14-inch rifles', drained the water from the water-cooled .50 calibers, and fired those until the barrels burned out. They threw their rifles into the bay and stacked the disabled machine guns in a pile. At least, Mac thought, the Japanese wouldn't be able to use them on U.S. forces when American troops returned to the Philippines

They sat down and waited, many asking just how long they would have to wait before transport to Corregidor. There wasn't much anyone could say. Mac sat there and looked around at his buddies—dirty, dusty and exhausted. Many of them were crying and still others were showing early signs of the ailments they'd be living with in the weeks, months and years ahead.

Shortly before the surrender order came from General Wainwright, Corporal Irving Strobing of Brooklyn, New York, a telegrapher in Malinta Tunnel, pounded out a final message to ships at sea and anyone else listening on that frequency. Strobing, like all the others, was exhausted and disoriented from the thousands of shells that had rained down on Corregidor. Here is part of what he tapped out on the telegraph key:

> Notify any and all vessels headed toward this area to return to their home ports. They are not here yet. We are waiting for God only knows what … Lots of heavy firing going on. We've only got about an hour and twenty minutes before … we may have to give up about noon. We've got about 55 minutes and I feel sick at my stomach. I'm really low down. They bring in the wounded every minute. We will be waiting for you guys to help. This is the only thing I guess can be done. General Wainwright is an all-right guy and we are willing to go on for him, but shells were dropping all night, faster than hell. Damage terrific. Too much for guys to take—men here all feeling bad because of terrific strain of the siege. Corregidor used to be a nice place, but it's haunted now … can't think at all. I can hardly think. They are piling all the dead and wounded in our tunnel. Arms weak from pounding key long hours, no rest, short rations, tired …. I know how a mouse feels. Caught in a trap waiting for guys to come along and finish up. My name is Irving Strobing. Get this to my mother, Mrs. Minnie Strobing, 605 Barbey Street, Brooklyn, New York. Message… my love to Pa, Joe, Sue, Mac, Joy and Paul … also to my family and friends. Tell Joe, wherever he is, to give 'em hell for us. My love to you all. God bless you and keep you. Sign my name and tell my mother how you heard from me. Stand by ….

That was the last message out of Corregidor.

When the sun was high enough in the sky, Japanese soldiers in motor launches came ashore on Ft. Hughes to round up their American prisoners. Mac, his buddies and the rest of the men on the little island, their hands clasped together on top of their heads, walked toward the shoreline and surrendered. Sad, but with heads unbowed, the prisoners were pushed and prodded by the Japanese soldiers as they came down from their positions in the rocks. They boarded the launches for the short ride to Corregidor and the 92nd Maintenance Garage, a former PBY landing area which was large enough to hold all Corregidor's prisoners of war—about 7,000 American and 14,000 Filipino soldiers. Sadly, so many of the men and women who were on, or made it to, Corregidor were non-combatants or service personnel who provided services other than squeezing a trigger or pulling the lanyard of a canon. These were the people who populated the tunnels of Corregidor, and it was a thin line of troops—Navy, Marine, Army and Filipinos—outside the tunnel that had been battling the Japanese on the beach. Some of those fighting on the beach had received no more than a few hours' instruction on how to aim and fire a rifle.

Corporal Glenn McDole, like all the others on Corregidor, had been fighting the Japanese from a distance. Now, he was facing the enemy up close, and he was beginning to hate them. His hatred for them would increase a hundred-fold in the years ahead. The cocky young Marine had a lot to learn about his captors. Mac stood in line in the garage area where Japanese soldiers were taking their names, rank and serial numbers. They were searched as they walked into the building, and Mac was certain he'd come out of the building without his watch, wallet or other personal items. He quickly shoved his Urbandale High School class ring in his mouth, thinking that at least he'd have that.

He stepped up to the table where he told a little Japanese guard, "Glenn W. McDole, Corporal, United States Marine Corps, Serial Number 301051." Three guards stepped up from behind him and took his watch. When they took his wallet, his temper flared and he grabbed for it and screamed, "Damn it! Give me that back!" Mac wanted the family pictures in his wallet. One of the guards hit him from behind with a club, and he dropped to his knees. He lost all reason, and all he could think of was "getting back at those sons of bitches." He got up on all fours, ready to charge at the Jap who'd hit him, when he saw the three other guards standing there, smiling and slapping their billy clubs against the palms of their hands, waiting for him to make a move. He realized then that he couldn't win. He got up off the floor, brushed himself off and walked out to the holding area with a firm commitment to not let those bastards take away his pride or his spirit. He still had the class ring in his mouth.

That was Mac's first encounter with a Japanese soldier who had been indoctrinated at an early age with "Bushido," or the warrior's code. Since the 16th century, Bushido had been deeply ingrained in all levels of Japanese society, starting with the Samurai, or military class. It called for a martial spirit which stressed courage in battle and serving one's Emperor until death. To a Japanese warrior, suicide was preferable to surrender, and those who did surrender were treated with utter contempt. Under Bushido, compassion was a weakness, and they followed the code to the letter throughout the Pacific War. The Japanese enlisted man was well prepared psychologically to commit the beatings, torture and executions that took place. The treatment he received during training in the Japanese Imperial Army was brutal and sadistic, and he passed it down to his captives. Mac, Smitty and Henderson would be among the thousands who suffered.

The Burial Details

For two days, the young Iowan and all the others in the garage area went without food or water. There was no shelter from the Philippine sun, no latrines, no building of any sort, just thousands of men crammed into an area 1,500 yards by 800 yards. The garage area had one water pump, and it was nearly impossible to get to because of the tremendously long lines.

For the sick and dying, there was no medical treatment, so the POW doctors resorted to whatever crude methods they could devise to treat them. The long siege on Corregidor had taken a toll, and it was beginning to show in the number of men dropping from malaria, dysentery, or lack of food and water. There were no latrines in the garage area for the thousands of prisoners, so straddle trenches were dug in an effort to solve the sanitation problem. It didn't help. The exposed trenches increased the spread of dysentery. The stench was overwhelming, and because of it, Japanese guards wouldn't enter the prison compound.

On the third day of his stay inside the garage area, Mac received his first food—a can of Carnation milk, which he had to share with two other prisoners. He was to receive a third of a can of Carnation milk as his daily food ration for the remainder of his stay on Corregidor. By now, the young Marine wasn't the 185-pound athlete he'd been during his days at the Cavite Navy Yard. Life under fire for weeks on end, powdered eggs and beans as his main diet at Ft. Hughes, and now a meager amount of milk a day as his only food was causing a weight loss. He was exhausted. He held his portion of milk in his hand after the two other prisoners had had their share, and looked for a place to sit down, rest and drink.

As he searched, he spotted two dirty, skinny Marines sunning themselves on a rock. They looked familiar, but he wasn't sure until he walked up closer and squinted. Then came recognition from both sides as Rufus Smith and Roy Henderson got up off the rock and ran toward Mac, who was already moving toward them. Smitty, in a slow Texas drawl said, "Dole, ya ol' rascal, where in hell ya been?" Mac, who had missed that drawl since their separation at the Navy Yard, replied with, "Takin' in the sights, my friend, just been takin' in the sights!" They held out their right hands to shake and, at the same time, their left hands grabbed each other on the shoulders and they embraced. Both had tears in their eyes as they stood there. "My God," thought Mac, "He looks bad. Do I look that bad to him?" He did.

The three sat down and talked about what had happened to them. After the destruction of the Navy Yard in Cavite, both Smitty and Roy had been sent to Corregidor. They had been there since shortly after Mac left for Los Baños. Mac told them about Squeaky Myrick getting killed on Ft. Hughes. Then talk turned to what might be in store them in the days ahead. They had already seen evidence of what the Japanese were capable of doing to prisoners. They concluded there were bad times ahead of them.

It wasn't long before working parties were formed to clean up the island, and there was plenty to be done. The bodies of American, Japanese and Filipino soldiers were everywhere; the stench of death overpowered prisoners sent out under guard to pick up dead Japanese soldiers. They were stacked like cordwood, soaked in a flammable substance and then burned. Their ashes were then portioned out in small containers for the trip back to Japan. Decay and its sickening odor came quickly in the tropics and with their meager diet of a half can of milk a day, there was little the prisoners could heave up when they became sick. They never got used to the smell of death.

The Filipino and American bodies were next but, by that time, they were bloated and black from exposure to the Philippine sun. The prisoners managed to dig one large shallow grave, where they placed their fallen comrades and covered them with what little soil there was on the island. They were not allowed to remove the dog tags from the bodies of the American and Filipino soldiers. The grave was unmarked, and the Japanese wouldn't allow a military service. All the burial detail could do was whisper a quick prayer and move on.

There were other jobs. After all the bodies had been disposed of, there was scrap metal and other debris to be picked up and hauled down to ships at the landing. All the metal would go back to Japan to be melted down. While Mac picked it up under the hot Philippine sun, other work parties went about taking the tons of food and medical supplies from Mal-

Corporal Glenn McDole with his mother, Dessa, shortly after he returned from Washington, D.C., where he told military justice officials what had happened on Palawan Island.

inta Tunnel and hauling it down to the shore to be loaded onto still more Japan-bound ships. The sick, wounded and disabled among the Americans and Filipinos on the island were left without so much as a Band-Aid.

The Telegram

While Corporal Glenn McDole was picking up the dead and the debris of war, back home in Iowa his mother received the telegram that *was* to have been sent after the bombings at the Cavite Navy Yard some five months earlier. It was Mother's Day when Dessa McDole read the message:

> The Commandant, U.S. Marine Corps regrets to advise you that according to the records of this headquarters, your son, Private First Class Glenn McDole, U.S. Marine Corps, was performing his duty in the service of his country in the Manila Bay area when the station capitulated. He will be carried on the records of the Marine Corps as missing, pending further information. No report of his death has been received and he may be a prisoner of war. It will probably be several months before definite official information can be expected concerning his status. Sincere sympathy is extended you in your anxiety and you are assured that any report received will be communicated to you promptly.
>
> Sincerely,
> T. Holcomb, Lieutenant Gen. USMC
> Commandant, U.S. Marine Corps.

At the McDole home in Iowa, Dessa McDole told Mac's brothers and sisters—Max, Joe, Colleen, Margaret and Dolores—that she knew Glenn was okay. The close-knit McDoles never gave up hope. They figured he was alive because of the cablegram he'd sent on Christmas Eve. The next day, they all sat down and wrote Mac a letter telling him that they missed him, loved him and were praying for his safe return. They hoped their letter would get to the young Marine.

3

On the Move

On May 24, 1942, eighteen days after American forces surrendered on Corregidor, the POWs were told to move out. Gathering up what little belongings they had, Mac and the others started their walk to the transport ships at Bottomside. Once there, Japanese soldiers forced them, at bayonet point, into the ship's holds, where they were told to stand at attention. Then began the process of cramming as many humans as possible into the ship. When it was finished, they were so tightly packed that not a man could move. The hatch was slammed shut, and the battle-weary survivors were plunged into darkness. Behind them, Corregidor, void of vegetation from the thousands of shells and bombs that had hit it, showed no signs of American occupation. The Japanese flag had replaced Old Glory on Topside, and the 14-inch rifles, huge mortars, machine guns and other weapons of war were nothing more than scrap metal on board ships bound for Japan, to be melted down to make more guns and bullets for the Japanese war effort.

Once underway, it took less than a half-hour to cover the distance between Corregidor and Manila, and when the ship pulled as close to shore as it could without beaching, the Japanese guards forced all the prisoners into the water. Those too sick to walk and too weak to swim drowned when they were pushed into neck-deep water just a few yards from shore. Carrying a few meager possessions—his empty canteen, a canvas sea bag with a blanket, his poncho, mess kit, Bible and helmet—Mac helped the weaker prisoners as best he could, but some were beyond help. He made it to shore with Smitty and Henderson, where they were met by screaming guards who formed them into a long column, four abreast, for the march to Bilibid Prison. The dead floated to shore.

Mac and the other GIs who marched down Dewey Boulevard that day would later call it "The Gloat March." The Japanese wanted to humiliate the defeated army, but their plan backfired. Japanese soldiers on horseback kept the prisoners in a straight line while marching down the boulevard but, instead of anger and catcalls, the prisoners were met by cheers from the Filipino men, women, and children who crowded the sidewalks. Often, a Filipino woman would run into the street, having recognized a loved one. They would embrace, and then, as if on cue, a saber-wielding horseman would run them down. Blood flowed as the prisoners marched toward Bilibid, but those who lined the streets cheered for the defeated army. Some Filipino prisoners managed to break ranks and escape into the crowd, while civilians tossed food to the starving prisoners. Mac and his buddies caught hunks of brown sugar thrown by Filipino women. Others threw fruit and balutes (a partially incubated chicken egg the Filipinos considered a delicacy) and, occasionally, a drink of water so badly needed by the hundreds of dehydrated war prisoners.

The march was murderous. Many of the prisoners, seriously ill or suffering from wounds, staggered along the five-mile route to Bilibid. It could have been accomplished much sooner had the Japanese used the more direct route, roughly two miles, but one of their objectives was to let the Filipinos know that American influence in the Philippines had ended.

The march continued up the boulevard, with the heat of the midday sun draining what little energy the prisoners had left. When a prisoner staggered out of line or fell, Mac, Smitty, Henderson and other prisoners who had the energy carried them for as long as they could. But when they became too weak to carry any further, they dropped them alongside the curb. The Japanese cavalrymen told the prisoners to move on, that a truck would pick up the stragglers. When they'd marched on a few yards, they would hear the crack of a rifle. They didn't look back. They knew, however, what had happened: one less prisoner to feed; one too weak to work, anyway.

There had been no other scene like it since the Bataan Death March nearly two months before—the exhausted and wounded dropping by the wayside while foot soldiers ran through the lines with fixed bayonets, to keep the prisoner lines straight and moving. But the longer they marched, the more food was thrown into their ranks, and the applause and yells of encouragement shown by the Filipino men and women lining the parade route made the Japanese soldiers furious. They vented their anger on both the prisoners and the civilians lining Dewey Boulevard. It was a ghastly day. The Japanese Cavalry slashed and shot its way up Dewey Boulevard. Mac couldn't remember how long it took to make the five-mile walk to

Bilibid. He figured it took several hours, but no one could give a precise time. There wasn't a watch among the thousands of prisoners, because all their personal items had been taken by the Japanese.

Bilibid Prison in Manila was the Philippine Alcatraz. Only hard-core Filipino criminals—murderers, rapists and thieves—were housed at Bilibid, and that was one of the reasons all the POWs were marched to the prison: to show that the American and Filipino POWs were no better than those already behind bars at Bilibid. Mac, Smitty and Roy were among the thousands who filed slowly into the big prison. Its 17 acres were surrounded by solid walls of masonry, some 6-feet thick and about 20-feet high. In the center was a huge circular guard tower, and the cell blocks spread out from the tower to form what appeared to be spokes on a wheel. Other guard towers were placed on the prison walls, making Bilibid escape-proof. The sick and wounded were taken inside the buildings where a makeshift hospital was set up. The rest of Corregidor's survivors stayed outside, where they waited in long lines to drink or to fill their canteens from the yard's two water faucets. Mac learned to drink sparingly at Bilibid. It was there that Mac, Smitty and Roy made a pact which none of them would break. They would share water, food and any other item to stay alive. "What's mine is yours, and what's yours is mine," they said, and their pact would prove to be a lifesaver.

Shortly after they arrived at Bilibid, they ate their first meal since the surrender. For the nearly two weeks of life as a POW on Corregidor, they had survived on a third of a can of Carnation milk a day. Mac and all the others were losing weight at an alarming rate. His first meal at Bilibid was a rice ball, perhaps a half-step up from the canned milk. The rice balls were about the size of a baseball. There was no flavor, no meat in them, just rice molded into a ball. As he took his first bite of the rice ball, Mac looked at Smitty and said, "It sure beats what we were used to, which was nothing." From then on, food, or the lack of it, was on their minds constantly. They went to sleep at night dreaming about food and woke up hungry and thinking of food, every day.

A cold rain came down in sheets the first night at Bilibid, and the prisoners ran for cover inside the four ancient prison buildings. There wasn't much protection from the rain. The roofs leaked, and to keep warm the three of them wrapped themselves in their blankets. Those who didn't have blankets walked from cell to cell begging and hoping that someone would share their blanket and body warmth.

They spent a week in Bilibid, sitting outside doing nothing but talking, and it gave them time to regain some of the energy expended during the long battle of Corregidor and the cleanup of the island following their surrender. They squatted, hunched in a circle, and talked about home, their families and their lives before the Marines. To break the monotony, they'd get a group together and sing, but when it came to music, Mac was a tin-eared singer who couldn't have carried a tune in his sea bag. He was booed so much that he soon quit singing. Those were the only good moments at Bilibid, and while they talked of home and sang, the ranks of the able-bodied were thinning. Men were dying in the prison's hospital, and more and more of them dropped from malaria. The Japanese had confiscated all the quinine used to prevent the attacks. There were many other deadly maladies associated with the tropics and their near-starvation diet—pellagra, beriberi, scurvy—all associated with vitamin deficiencies. Adding to the suffering was a host of funguses and skin ailments, which could not be treated properly, because what few doctors there were had no medicines, not so much as an aspirin or a Band-Aid. Disease was to be a constant companion to all the prisoners in the Philippines. However, Mac was lucky: so far he hadn't come down with any of the debilitating diseases. Although near exhaustion and having lost some weight, he was still in fairly good shape. As a POW on Corregidor, he had managed to steal a large bottle of quinine tablets while on a work party inside the Malinta Tunnel. So far, the guards hadn't discovered it or his high school class ring in his nearly empty sea bag. He'd have some relief if he should come down with malaria, and he'd share it with Smitty and Henderson when they came down with it.

The sun rose over Manila, and it promised to be another hot, humid day. Mac and the others were waking up, anticipating another day of inactivity when, suddenly, Japanese troops entered the prison yard screaming "Kuda! Kuda!" ("Get a move on!"), and moved them out of the prison into the street, where the prisoners were ordered to form into another long column. They had no idea, no word of where they might be headed, but there was another long walk ahead of them to the Manila train depot. Word of the march quickly spread through the city, and again Filipino men and women lined the streets to continue their barrage of food: rice balls, lumps of brown sugar and balutes. As the still healthy walked and ate, the sick and wounded began to drop. Some of them would never get up, but the column continued its march through Manila, where it finally halted at the city's train depot.

They wondered what was in store for them, where they were headed and how long it would take. As the sun rose higher in the sky and the heat of the day bore down, they were told to line up alongside a freight train consisting of fifteen boxcars. The engine and metal boxcars ran on narrow-gauge tracks, just as they did in much of Europe. It was accepted that during World War I, a narrow-gauge boxcar could hold about forty men or eight horses. That wasn't enough for the Japanese, and they intended to set a new record for the number of men packed into what would become steel coffins. The Japanese achieved a new level of inhumanity in doing so.

They screamed, "Kuda! Kuda!" as they pushed and packed the prisoners into the cars so tightly they couldn't move, could not even raise their arms. A boxcar that normally held 40 men now held over a hundred, but Mac and his buddies lucked out: They were the last to be shoved inside their car, which left them near the door. The door slammed shut and the prisoners began screaming and yelling. The heat inside the darkened metal car was suffocating, the luckless prisoners shoved up against the metal sides of the car screamed in pain, as if they'd been thrown up against a huge heated cooking griddle. The screaming was deafening, and the guards finally opened the door just wide enough for some daylight to enter, but it didn't force any more air into the car. Mac had a hard time breathing as he yelled at the guard stationed at the partially opened door, "Open the door all the way so we can get some air in here, or we'll throw your ass out of here!" Whether he understood English or not, the guard got the message and opened the door wide enough to get some air in the car, but it did nothing to alleviate the heat or produce much of an air flow. Some men in the super-heated boxcars were now beginning to die, but no one knew it. Some of the prisoners were dead on their feet, propped up by the press of flesh against flesh. Mac, Smitty and Henderson, standing at the door, managed to kneel down and tried to fan air into the back of the boxcar, but it did little to reduce the combined stench of sweat, urine, shit and death.

The train inched its way north out of Manila and headed for Cabanatuan, about 60 miles from the city. The Japanese had set up two prisoner of war camps near the town. It was here that Corregidor's prisoners would be reunited with some of their comrades from Bataan. It would take all day to cover the distance, and there were no rest stops, food or water. No attempts were made by the prisoners to escape by jumping from the train, because machine gunners were stationed atop each boxcar.

Somehow, word spread in the countryside that a prisoner of war train was coming through, and at each little village along the way the tracks were lined with villagers who threw food to the prisoners—once again, a shower of sugar blocks, eggs, bread and rice cookies. Mac watched as Filipino men, women and children ran up to the car and handed them food before being struck by the guard standing in the boxcar doorway. He managed to catch the biggest block of brown sugar he'd ever laid eyes on. He split it three ways with Smitty and Roy. Smitty caught some rice bread, which he shared with Mac and Roy, and then it was time to share what other food they caught with the rest of the prisoners. They threw the food to the back of the car where tightly packed prisoners, if able to move at all, might snag a piece of bread, some rice cookies or sugar.

The train chugged into Cabanatuan that night, and again the curses and commands of the Japanese soldiers could be heard as the prisoners were herded off the train and lined up in formation. Mac suffered his first wound in his second encounter with a Japanese soldier when he was stabbed in the back with a bayonet while jumping from the boxcar. It was a deep wound which cut into the left side of his back just below the rib cage. The blood spurted as Mac started running toward the guard, while other soldiers, bayonets fixed, turned to meet him as he moved forward. He was mad as hell and flat-out wanted a piece of the Jap. He was about halfway there and hoping for a chance at throttling the little bastard when Smitty ran up from behind and pulled him back. "Your temper is gonna get you killed, Dole!" he hissed. Smitty kept pushing him away from the scene and with a stern whisper said, "You've got to start controlling it, or you'll never make it through this!"

Mac knew Smitty was right. His temper had shown again, and he knew he'd probably been saved from something far worse than a bayonet wound when Smitty intervened. His back was still bleeding, and he wanted Smitty to take a look at it, but Smitty had gone on ahead. Filipino towns-people had shown up at their arrival in Cabanatuan, and one of them, see-ing Mac's wound, threw him a block of salt and motioned to put it on his wound. He tried to reach it, but couldn't get to it. Then one of the other prisoners came up from behind and told him to keep walking. As they walked about four city blocks to a school yard, the prisoner lifted Mac's torn shirt, wiped off the blood and began rubbing salt into the wound. It burned, and Mac figured it had to be working at cleaning out the wound. He kept walking and, as the blood continued to flow down his back, the prisoner behind would wipe off the flow with Mac's shirt and then rub more salt into the wound.

When they arrived at a school yard, they were told they'd be spend-ing the night there. The Japanese had placed a huge kettle in the center of the yard, and rice was being cooked for the prisoners. There were so many prisoners, about 1,500 of them, and the line to the rice kettle so long that many of the men, exhausted from the day's hellish ride in the boxcars, sat down and made no attempt to eat. Those who did received only a mea-ger amount, less than half a mess kit. It was a pathetic scene in the school yard as the sick and exhausted prisoners silently gobbled up their tiny ration. Cabanatuan had been called the "Rice Bin of the Philippines." Thousands of tons of rice were stored there, enough to feed any army for months on end, and it did. It fed the Japanese Imperial Army.

The best part of that day came at dusk, when it began to rain. The prisoners were filthy. They hadn't had any water all day, and when the wind picked up and a heavy downpour began, it felt good. It was like taking a shower, and Mac felt a lot better. He rubbed the rain over his body, and he lifted his head skyward, opened his mouth and caught the first water he'd had all day. It was his first drink since Bilibid Prison. But the longer it rained, the colder he became and, before long, he sought protection and warmth from his poncho and blanket.

Mac finally spotted Smitty and yelled for him to come over. "Where in hell did you go?" Mac yelled. Smitty walked over to Mac and said, "Listen, my friend, we're in this together, but I'm not about to get myself killed because of your damned Irish temper. If you'd have clobbered that guard for what he did, the other sons-of-bitches would have killed ya'. Then I would have tried to kill one of them. There's no way we can overpower these Japs. You know that and so do they, so we've got to stay cool!" Mac lowered his head and apologized saying, "I know Smitty, I know. I just can't help it sometimes!" Smitty wouldn't accept it. "By God you better start trying, Dole," he yelled, "that is, if you ever want to see your Mom again! If you don't care if you see her, or if you don't care about the hell she'll go through if you get yourself killed, then go ahead and try and beat these Japs single-handedly! Just leave me alone, 'cause I'm gonna' make it back home, with or without you!" Smitty started to walk away and Mac, even more apologetic, said "Damnit, Smitty, I know I was wrong. I'll control it, just stick with me. I'll prove to ya' I can do it." With Smitty's lecture and Mac's apology accepted, the two spent the night huddled together, their blankets used as tents to keep the steady rain off them. During the night, when it was quiet, the young Iowan took stock. He knew what Smitty had said was right, and from now on, he thought, the Japanese are not gonna get to me. Smitty made sense, and Mac did care about his mother and what she'd go through if he were killed. "I'll get home," he mumbled, "I know I will!"

Daybreak, and the prisoners were on the march again. Japanese soldiers screamed the now-familiar, "Kuda! Kuda!" as the prisoners formed up into columns and started marching. It was a slow march, made even more intolerable under scorching sun and the heat of the day. Many prisoners staggered and dropped to the ground along the road, which was lined with trucks carrying Japanese soldiers. The soldiers taunted the prisoners, spitting on them and occasionally using their bayonets to spur them to move faster. For Mac and others it was still another day of marching without a rest and no water to drink. But the Filipino villagers who lined the six-mile route to the prison camps once more ignored the Japanese guards, yelling encouragement and again throwing food to the hungry men.

The Cabanatuan prison camps could be seen at some distance. The terrain was flat, and there were no hills to block the view of a site that would be the final stop for thousands of prisoners. Many of them would die there. Mac felt the hair on the back of his neck stand up, and he was consumed by a new sense of helplessness and despair as he walked through the gate of Camp One. His first thought was that he was standing at the Gateway to Hell. Roy and Smitty were just as stunned at the sight of the camp. Bamboo huts, both large and small, were crammed into the camp, all of them encircled by an eight-foot barbed wire fence. Each large hut, 18 feet by 55 feet, would house 150 to 200 men. The smaller huts, 18 feet by 40 feet, would house 100 men each. Watch towers were everywhere, and the guards stationed on the towers had the necessary rifles and machine guns to stop any attempt at escape. Mac remembered his two boot camp drill instructors, Sgt. Heindale and Corporal Coffee, telling them the first thing to do if captured was to look for a means to escape. As he looked over Cabanatuan's Camp One, Mac knew there was no way out. He knew the three of them would just have to stick it out in that hell hole and make do with what they had.

The camp was an old, rotting Philippine Army barracks in need of repair. There was no attempt to make it any more livable than it was. They slept on bamboo floors; there were no cots or mats, no cover of any kind to keep dry from the rain, which leaked through a rotting roof, no mesh netting to keep out mosquitoes; and it was filthy. Rats and mice were everywhere, the bamboo floors were infested with lice, and there was one shower, but it took a doctor's permission to use it. There were other showers, but Japanese guards forbade their use because there was so little water. This would be Mac's new home, where the "Red Meatball" of the Japanese Empire fluttered atop a flag pole at the camp's main gate.

The first day at Camp One, Cabanatuan, all the prisoners were assigned to working parties. Mac was told to gather wood for fires while others built a galley in the middle of the camp. His work party, always under guard, found and cut wood outside the camp. The galley consisted of two big black pots placed on iron stands just high enough off the ground to keep the fires burning under them. Three big canvas lister bags, supported by a wood frame similar to an Indian teepee, each holding 50 to 200 gallons of water, were situated around the camp.

Mac ate his first Camp One meal, which consisted of a half-mess kit of rice laced with worms and bugs. He and many other prisoners thought the bugs and worms were the best and most nutritious part of the meal. After eating the first meal, Mac told Smitty and Henderson that, it being the first day at Cabanatuan, perhaps things would get better. The next day they were given the same meal again, and he knew then that it would not get any better. After the first day, they received two half-mess kits of rice a day, along with a weak cup of tea.

The three buddies watched as small work parties unloaded supplies for the Japanese and cleared rocks and other debris from inside the old Filipino Army base. When not assigned to work parties, they sat outside, the sun beating down on them, and talked about home and family. By this time they felt they knew everything about each other, so long-forgotten stories were dredged up and retold. They'd laughed at Mac's telling about the day he left for boot camp, when most of his senior class, including all his buddies on the football and basketball teams, showed up at the train station to see him off.

Mac admitted that he was a two-timer. He'd just stepped out of his brother Max's car, along with his Mom, brothers and sisters, when his buddy, Dave, came running up to him. "Mac," he said, "I've got some bad news for ya'." Mac pulled his travel bag out of the car and said, "Oh, what's that?" "Both Virginia Phillips and Betty Lathrop are here to see you off!" Mac's mouth dropped open, and his face flushed red. He looked around and then asked, "Where are they?" Dave pointed and said, "Virginia's right over there with some of her friends, and Betty is on the other side of the station waiting for you. It's supposed to be a surprise, I guess. Mac, I thought you had this all figured out!" "I thought so too," Mac mumbled, as he walked over to where all his classmates were standing. He thanked all of them for coming and then walked over to Virginia, and for the next few minutes it was sweet talk and fancy footwork as he maneuvered between the two girls. He hugged Virginia and gave her a kiss, telling her he'd miss her, and then mumbled an apology and said he'd be right back. He ran to the other side of the train station, where he said his sweet good-byes to Betty. Tears were running down Betty's cheeks and Glenn McDole, ever the tender heart, softly wiped them away with his handkerchief. "I'll miss you, and I promise to write as soon as I get there," he said. "You better," she whispered, as she reached up and gave him another kiss. Mac was getting very nervous. He figured Virginia might show up on that side of the station. He gave Betty another quick hug and told her he had to get over to his mom and his brothers and sisters.

As he ran back to the other side of the station, another buddy, Corky, was laughing at the mess he was in. "You'll need that long train ride to rest up from all this running back and forth, Glenn," said Corky. "You're a real smart-ass, Corky," Glenn said as he came up behind Virginia, wrapped his arms around her and said, "See, I wasn't gone long, was I?" Virginia started to cry as she told him how much she would miss him. He reached for his handkerchief to wipe away her tears and then thought better of it. There might be some of Betty's makeup on it, and how would he explain that?

He promised to write just as soon as he got to San Diego, and as he walked away, he stopped briefly to bid goodbye to his buddies. With that done, he walked over to his family just as the conductor yelled, "All aboard!" This was his toughest goodbye. He hugged his mother, Dessa, a little woman who Glenn thought was the toughest, most caring woman he'd ever known, a woman who had tirelessly raised six kids and never lost her temper with any of them. His dad, David, wasn't there to say goodbye. He was out of town working to support the family. Then, hugging his brothers, and with hugs and kisses for his sisters, he boarded the train for San Diego. As he retold the story again at Cabanatuan, it seemed so long ago.

In the European War only two percent of American and allied prisoners of war died in German prison camps. In the Pacific War, nearly forty out of a hundred prisoners died in Japanese prison camps.

Many of the American soldiers imprisoned at Camp One, Cabanatuan, would never leave. The diet of two half-servings of rice per day, weak tea and an occasional bowl of what the prisoners called mongo bean soup, as well as the untreated wounds of battle and the diseases—malaria, beriberi, scurvy, dysentery, dengue fever, and pellagra—began taking lives. Ten to fifteen men died every day at the camp. Camp doctors, like those at Bilibid or the other prison camps in the Philippines, could provide only primitive first aid. There were no drugs or medicines of any kind, and they lacked even bandages. Death was a constant companion. Most of those who died early on were those who had survived the Bataan Death March. Burial details were commonplace, but with the hundred of prisoners in the camp, Mac was never picked for a burial detail, he had done enough of that on Corregidor. So far, Mac, Smitty and Roy Henderson were free of disease. None of them had come down with malaria. All three took quinine pills from the big bottle Mac had managed to smuggle out of the hospital in Corregidor, but there weren't many pills left. None of the three had dysentery, which was debilitating to the already weakened POWs who had suffered through the long Bataan Death March to Camp O'Donnell and then to Cabanatuan.

The latrines were "straddle trenches," 15-feet long, six feet deep and three feet wide. Throughout the day and night there was a constant line of men waiting for a spot to open up along the trench. Many couldn't wait, and the results were obvious. When it rained, the ground around the trenches was mud, mixed with human waste, and there were many who lost their footing and fell in. Some prisoners, so weak they could hardly walk, sat down at the edge of the trenches to relieve themselves. To add to the outrage, the cooking area was located next to the latrines. The thousands of flies attracted to the camp made no distinction between the two areas and were a major factor in the spread of disease. For the time being, the main enemies in Camp One were disease and malnutrition, all brought about by the neglect and cruelty of the Japanese.

Mac could see the day-to-day changes in the condition of those around him. Some of them already looked like walking skeletons, their bones protruding from beneath taut skin, their eyes sunk into sockets, their gums receding due to scurvy. Overexposure to the sun and its blistering heat caused the weaker ones, those without any fat on their bodies, to have exposed bones protruding from their skin. The lighter skinned prisoners would burn, then blister, only to go through the same process over again. As bad and as evil as it was, Mac was heartened by the fact that most of the prisoners had a look in their eyes which showed a determined will to live. For some, that special look was gone, however. The light had dimmed, and Mac could tell which ones wouldn't be around much longer.

The simple routine at Camp One: up in the morning, sit in the sun all day, that is if you weren't on a work party, talk to your buddies and wait for your two half-meals, bury the dead if you were a member of a burial party, and then it was into the hut at dusk for the rest of the night. By now, it was clear to the three of them that to survive they'd have to find a way to get out of Camp One, into a work project that needed a small number of men. From that situation, they might not have to return to Cabanatuan. That was their goal, and they sought a better position to achieve it. They stayed near the front gate during the day. When Japanese soldiers entered the camp looking for prisoners physically strong enough for work projects, they would listen. If it would be a two- or three-day project, they would melt back into the crowd. They wanted something much longer. Time was running out. All three of them were losing weight. Meanwhile, the day-to-day routine in Camp One continued. Prisoners were dying from wounds or disease. The two half-meals per day continued. And they spent most of their time sitting under a blazing Philippine sun cursing the "Jap bastards" who guarded them. They had good reason to hate.

They were squatting near the front gate when guards marched four Americans, part of an outside work party, into the camp. The four claimed they'd lost their way but had found the road and were walking back to camp when soldiers picked them up. The guards began beating them. Everyone knew the penalty for attempted escape, and what happened next was only a prelude to the inevitable. The soldiers began beating them with sticks. They hit them and hit them and hit them again until the prisoners huddled from the blows in a bloody stupor. All the POWs who were watching stood in silent rage as the beatings continued. When they'd finished, the soldiers hog-tied the prisoners in such a way that almost any movement on their part would have strangled them. With the ropes in place they were left squatting in the prison yard for two days. Bloodied and beaten, the four begged for water, but had anyone moved to help them, there would have been a fifth prisoner squatting in the yard. Mac and the rest of the men in his hut had no sleep for two nights as they agonized over the cries of the prisoners begging for water, food and relief from the pain of bondage.

On the third day, the guards marched into the camp and untied the prisoners. They brought four shovels with them, and the prisoners were told to dig their own mass grave. They started digging as hundreds of American prisoners looked on. By now, the four men, resigned to what lay ahead, dug with quiet dignity as the sun beat down on them. With the grave completed, the prisoners stood at attention before their executioners, shunning an offer of blindfolds. Their gaze moved beyond the firing squad to their fellow POWs in the yard, and as if on command, they saluted those who would remain behind. The firing squad raised their rifles, shots rang out, and the four GIs crumpled to the bottom of the trench. A Japanese officer stepped forward and administered the final coup de grace, two shots to the head of each prisoner. It was over. The other POWs were ordered to fill in the grave.

Neither Mac, nor Smitty, nor Roy knew the name of the GI who was the next victim at Cabanatuan. He lost control one hot mid-July day in '42 and got into a fight with one of the guards. No formal execution this time. Guards grabbed the man, cut off his ears and nailed his hands to the camp gate. The guards made extra trips in and out of the gate, and when they pushed the gate open it would swing into the prison's barbed wire fence, puncturing the GIs back and legs again and again. He was nailed to the gate for three days without food or water, and on several occasions guards would come by, sit down at his feet drink some water and eat their lunch, taunting him even more. On the fourth day, he was taken down off the gate and dragged to a trench, where the guards ordered other GIs to throw him in and cover him with dirt. Was he dead when thrown into the trench? Mac, Smitty and Roy were told he wasn't. The men who had covered him with dirt said he was still breathing when the dirt was being shoveled in on top of him.

Witnessing the last prisoner execution gave added impetus to their efforts to get out of Camp One, and their opportunity finally came on July 24, 1942. A guard and interpreter came into the camp looking for 300 healthy men to form a work detail, which they said would last about three months. Spending their time at the front gate had paid off, and the three volunteered, even though they did not know where they were going or what they would be doing. They gathered what little belongings they had and, along with the other prisoners, were marched out of the camp and back to the city of Cabanatuan. Instead of heading to the train station, they were loaded aboard trucks, some Japanese-made, the remainder, captured U.S. Army GMCs. As they rode along the bumpy dirt roads toward Manila, Smitty was optimistic. "This is sure gonna be better, guys," he said, "since they're not making us march to the train depot and get back in those sweat boxes."

The trip to Manila took about three hours. They jumped off the trucks at the old Filipino barracks next to the docks at Manila Harbor. Mac took a look around. The docks were in fairly good condition and, although the living conditions weren't the best, he thought it was a hell of a lot better than Cabanatuan's Camp One. The prisoners, all 300 of them, were put to work loading two small transport ships with picks, shovels, wheelbarrows, tons of bulk cement, rice and other food items for their three-month work project.

The cement was shoveled into huge canvas cargo sacks, which were then lowered into the holds and dumped. The two ships could best be described as inter-island type vessels but, small as they were, they carried quite a considerable load of cargo and passengers. It took a week of backbreaking shoveling and loading before the work ended, but McDole couldn't have been happier to see it over. He'd spent most of his time below deck, where the cement dust was so thick and the heat so intense he could hardly breathe. With loading complete, Mac, Smitty and Roy boarded the Santo Maru, still not knowing what their final destination was.

As the ship sailed out of Manila Harbor, taking a south by southwest course into the Sulu Sea, they sailed past Corregidor, now a barren piece of rock—foliage blasted away by thousands of bombs and shells, with no sign of life. They didn't say much as they sailed past the island, but they thought about the hundreds of American and Filipino soldiers who died there, many of them friends. Mac couldn't help thinking about Squeaky Myrick, his remains, or what remains there were, buried somewhere on Ft. Hughes. They didn't say anything, but all three gave The Rock a quick salute as they were herded down into the holds below deck. They remained there throughout the voyage, only leaving the hold to work in the ship's galley. The first day's meal aboard ship was rice, seaweed soup and mongo beans, and Smitty was delighted. "We're certainly gonna eat better wherever we're going," he drawled. "This is the smartest thing we could have ever done." Although things were shaping up a lot better than they'd anticipated, they remembered the evil the Japanese were capable of. The three of them, focused only on survival, knew they could never let their guard down.

Their second day out, the ship dropped anchor off Culion, a small island, one of over 7,000 in the Philippine chain. A guard picked Mac,

Smitty and Roy to be part of the work party hauling supplies to the island's inhabitants, all of them patients of the Culion Leper Colony. The barge's first load consisted mostly of disinfectant, and when they landed, the three sprayed the landing area with the disinfectant while the Japanese guards waited on the barge. Not one of the guards would go ashore until the entire area had been sprayed. Mac and the others in the work party couldn't help laughing at this. The guards, proud warriors of the Japanese Empire, were so frightened at the thought of catching leprosy that they made the prisoners spray the area before they felt safe enough to step ashore. With the spraying completed, Mac and the others began unloading food and other supplies.

A Catholic Priest, an American, was the islander's shepherd. He came down to the shore to greet the prisoners who unloaded the supplies and, without creating too much attention, walked among them praying and whispering over and over again, just loud enough to be heard, "Keep up the courage. God is with you." It wasn't long before the lepers—men, women and children—began showing up in ones and twos, and as they watched the prisoners unloading the supplies from the barge, they slowly moved in closer. In broken English they told the prisoners they, too, were praying for them.

It was an unbelievable sight for Mac. Men, women and children, covered with huge, oozing sores and seemingly unconcerned about their own fate, offered prayers and encouragement to the American prisoners. The captives were overwhelmed by the kind words and attention they received from the lepers and their families, many of whom had only partial faces, some of whom had lost a hand or a leg. Yet those castoffs wanted the prisoners to know they were concerned about their well-being. The sight sickened Mac, and yet, horrible as it was, the concern and love shown by the lepers for the young Americans buoyed his spirit. He would always remember the people of the Culion Leper Colony.

They had spent about two hours ashore and had completed the job. Guards hustled the prisoners back on the barge. As they headed to the ship, they looked back to see the priest and the lepers on the shoreline waving goodbye. Some were still praying. Mac wanted to know why the Japanese were showing so much concern for the lepers of Culion; they certainly hadn't shown any concern for the thousands they had captured on Corregidor and Bataan. This act of kindness by the Japanese seemed completely out of character. He asked the Japanese interpreter why they gave food and aid to the Culion lepers. He never got an answer.

When they climbed back aboard ship, an interpreter told the prisoners they were going to be part of a road-building detail on Palawan Island. "You will be fed American food," he said, "and, all in all, things will be very enjoyable." There were smiles and murmurs among the prisoners, Mac included, but the smiles on the prisoners' faces were as phony as the interpreter's comments. Not a man on board believed what they'd just heard. They knew they'd be stuck with wormy rice and hard labor for the duration, but it was still a helluva lot better than Cabanatuan, where by October of 1942 3,000 Americans had died from malnutrition, war wounds, and the brutal treatment of the prison guards.

4

Palawan Island

August 12, 1942

The *Santo Maru* and the other transport ship sailed into Palawan Harbor and dropped anchor mid-afternoon, completing a 334-mile ocean voyage. The hard work of loading the ships for the trip to Palawan and the meager rice diet were beginning to weaken the prisoners. They were marched into the village of Puerto Princesa and bedded down in an old Filipino Constabulary barracks. Vacant and in need of extensive repair, the barracks would be home for most of the 300 prisoners for nearly two and a half years. There were no cheers from the villagers, no food thrown at them when they walked through the village to the constabulary. The town was nearly deserted. The villagers had disappeared into the mountains when the Japanese landed on the island.

Of the 7,100 islands making up the Philippines, Palawan was one of the larger, stretching 270 miles north to south, with a mountain range down the center. It averaged only about 15 miles wide. Palawan was situated between two seas, the Sulu Sea on the east coast, and the South China Sea on the west. As for climate, islanders living along the western coast and on the northern and southern tips of Palawan endured a six-month rainy season. On the east coast, where Mac, Smitty and Henderson put to work, there was no pronounced rainy season, but there was a one- to three-month dry season. The climate fitted in nicely for the hard work they didn't yet know lay ahead.

First things first. They unloaded two ships and made major repairs on the barracks they'd be living in during the months ahead. The barracks was U-shaped, with its main gate facing the east. Stone pillars marked the

An Army Air Force reconnaissance plane took this photograph of the crowded Puerto Princesa Harbor (U.S. War Department).

entrance, and about a dozen coconut trees lined a road which began at the front gate and ran through the courtyard. A veranda provided some shade for the building, which looked out on the courtyard. For prisoners who broke the rules, there was a small jail in the corner of the barracks at the front gate. And, unlike the prisoner huts at Cabanatuan, Palawan's barracks had metal roofs and wood floors, but they had been vacant for a long time and needed a lot of work to make them livable.

The prisoners were divided into groups of ten with one guard assigned to each group. One group built a guard tower in the prison courtyard next to the barracks on the front side of the camp. About the height of a big Iowa windmill, the tower easily accommodated two guards and a machine gun. For added security, an eight-foot, double-entwined, barbed wire fence surrounded the camp, and a 60-foot cliff, which slanted precipitously to the coral rocks, guarded access to the bay below.

Under constant guard, Mac, Smitty, Roy and other prisoners were sent out to scavenge the deserted village for building material and any tools they could find. They competed with Japanese soldiers, who were also scouring the village looking for anything they could use to improve liv-

The only entrance into the Palawan Barracks prison camp. There were more attempted escapes from Palawan Barracks than any other prison camp in the Pacific (U.S. War Department).

ing conditions in their barracks, located outside the barbed wire about a half-block northeast of the prison.

Once the scavenging was complete, the prisoners set to work improving living conditions. It took a little over a week for the three hundred prisoners to make all the necessary repairs. The old barracks were cleaned, floors scrubbed, the sagging veranda was strengthened, and wood steps leading up to the barracks were replaced. The galley, which consisted of a large black pot resting on a brick base, and the prisoner's tea barrel were covered by a thatched roof, which provided much-needed shade for the prisoners assigned to work in the hot, steamy galley.

Next came the sanitation work. They dug trenches for the latrines, and were free to build them any way they wanted. Remembering the stench and filth of Bilibid prison and the POW camp at Cabanatuan, they laid boards across the trenches as seats and added a board below for a foot rest. It was a privy the POWs would find back home, but at least there would be no more slipping and falling into the trench on rainy days.

Inside the barracks, each man was responsible for his own bunk. Some prisoners used left-over lumber and interwoven bamboo for their beds. From the scavenging in the village, others found old doors, which they used as bunks. Mac felt the doors were so old and bug infested that it would be healthier to sleep on the floor, which was just what they did. Smitty and Roy joined Mac on the floor, using their folded blankets as a mattress, and the Japanese even provided ceiling-to-floor mosquito netting, each one big enough to envelope ten men. They'd lower the net when everyone was in place at night and raise it at reveille. The mosquito netting wasn't an act of kindness on the part of the Japanese. They needed prisoners healthy enough to work, and the netting would help ward off malaria. By this time, Mac had run out of quinine pills, and it was only a matter of time before all three would come down with the disease.

The camp needed water, and the three friends were assigned to a ten-man plumbing detail. They left the camp and went up a mountain to tap water from the streams. It wasn't easy. They dragged and carried 20-foot long, 3-inch diameter pipes up the mountain and connected them, one-by-one, down the mountain and all the way back to the prison camp. It

Inside the deserted building at the Palawan prison camp where American prisoners slept. Many of them slept on the floor. Others used old doors or makeshift sleeping mats (U.S. War Department).

was backbreaking work, exhausting and painful at times, but they took special care in laying the pipes, because they knew if there was a break in the water line they'd be climbing back up the mountain with more pipe to repair it.

Up to this point, Corporal Glenn McDole had been shot at by strafing Japanese Zeros, had survived hundreds of artillery duels and bombings, and had been bayoneted and beaten by Japanese soldiers. He had survived, however, in fairly good condition. He still had his temper, but with Smitty nearby to keep him in line he hadn't had any more encounters with Japanese guards. In the days to come, there would be encounters. Mac's hatred of the Japanese had grown steadily since his capture, but there was one exception to his loathing, they had a guard nicknamed "Smiley." Smiley was the guard assigned to the plumbing crew. He was a short, plump, older man, maybe in his thirties, and he smiled constantly. Before Smiley put on the uniform of a Japanese soldier, he had been a sign painter in his hometown in Japan. His name was Kuta Schugota, and Mac later admitted, "In all honesty, he was a pretty nice guy." Smiley let the prisoners take breaks while connecting the water pipes on the mountainside, and he looked the other way when Mac or the others ate coconuts, bananas or papayas they found in the brush. Smiley didn't fit the mold of the hardened Japanese soldier who lived by the warrior's code of "Bushido." He never yelled at the prisoners, never struck them, and never screamed, "Kuda, Kuda," to get them moving. He merely escorted them to their job sites and watched over them. He had a pleasant disposition, and the smile was always there. He was a far cry from the other guards, who enjoyed screaming at and beating prisoners whenever they felt like it. While they laid water pipes to the prison and later to the airfield, Smiley would watch over them. About every hour and a half, he'd say, in Japanese, "Mr. McDole, get rest! Go get some coconuts." Mac would scurry over to a coconut tree, climb it and knock the coconuts to the ground and then carry them to the others working at the project. Smiley also looked the other way when the prisoners ran across papayas. However, they were never allowed to carry them into the camp. "Forbidden fruit," according to Smiley. The camp commandant would have had them beaten for bringing food into the prison.

When they completed work on the water pipelines and returned to camp, they placed a large storage barrel over the latrines. When the water lines were hooked up, they were able to flush their waste into the ocean and to the camp's garbage pile located on the beach below the camp. They flushed the waste every three days, which helped control the flies and the smell. The sanitation system was as important for the Japanese as it was for the prisoners. It wasn't a humanitarian concern. They wanted healthy prisoners, because dysentery and other diseases related to climate and poor sanitation would cut into the number of men fit to complete the building project. Mac, along with the other 299 men in the camp, knew that if they were to survive, personal hygiene would be a top priority. There was a concerted effort by all the prisoners to make sure mess kits, barracks, and bodies were clean. After eating, coconut husks and ashes were used to scour mess kits. Blankets, for those prisoners who still had them, were draped over the porch railings to hang in the sun during the day, warding off parasites.

Reveille was at 6:00 every morning. Guards entered the building, yelling and kicking at the prisoners to get them up and out on the parade ground for the daily ritual of counting off and exercises. Once the guards had been assured that no prisoner had escaped during the night, the inmates were given a few minutes of calisthenics—not much, because there was work to be done. Then they stood at attention while the guards went through their daily ceremony of mock swordplay, saluting the Emperor and raising the "Red Meatball" up the camp's flagpole. This irritated the hell out of Mac and the others. They felt they had wasted a half-hour on Bushido ritual when they could have been eating. When they first arrived at Puerto Princesa, they were fed a mess kit of rice twice a day, but there would be a steady decrease in the amount of food they received each day. Nobody bothered to dig the worms or bugs out of the rice. They just ate them. Occasionally, they were given a side dish of camote vines, the Philippine version of the sweet potato. The guards ate the potatoes and the prisoners ate the boiled potato vines. After the morning meal they were given a vitamin tablet. "Make you strong," the Japanese said. All the prisoners wanted to work, because if they became sick or disabled and couldn't work, they received only a half-mess kit of rice twice a day, just enough to keep a man alive. It wasn't long after they arrived on the island that Smitty, then Henderson, and finally, Mac, came down with malaria. Their first malarial attack put them down on their sleeping mats for three to four days, but after that they did their best to get up and go to work after the first day of the attack. Food was more important to them than the high fever and chills, and if they lay in the barracks, they knew they would receive half of their daily rations.

Mac was a pack rat. He collected all the little boxes the prisoner's vitamin tablets came in. He wasn't a smoker and traded his weekly ration of ten cigarettes for items other prisoners had which might make him or his two survival buddies more comfortable.

By now, all of them knew who was in charge inside the compound. Army Captain Fred Bruni of Janesville, Wisconsin, was the man the prisoners answered to if they stepped out of line inside the barbed wire. That is the way the Japanese operated the camps. The guards stayed outside and entered the prison only when necessary. Another prisoner, Doctor Carl Mango of Harrisburg, Pennsylvania, held daily sick calls. He was the one who determined whether a man was too sick to work. Mac admired him more than any other officer in the camp, because he stood up to the Japanese. Mac believed Mango's support of the prisoners had impressed the guards, and even the camp's commanding officer, who appeared to have at least a grudging respect for the doctor. If a prisoner had a toothache, they depended on Doctor Henry Knight, a dentist from Portland, Oregon.

The camp even had a barber, John Warren, an army man from DeKalb, Mississippi, who shaped his barbering tools out of any metal he could find. The steel insole of an old army combat boot was his razor. He honed down its edge until it was nearly razor sharp. When prisoners scavenged the abandoned homes in Puerto Princesa, Warren found an old pair of clippers in one of the homes, and he set himself up in the barbering business, the same job he had had as a civilian. Mac was a regular customer. Like so many other prisoners, a beard drove him crazy. If he'd had any inclination to let his auburn hair grow, the Marine Corps had taught him there were fewer problems—no lice or other vermin to contend with—if one had close-cropped hair.

It took eight days for the inmates at Puerto Princesa to finish work on their barracks. On the ninth day, all 300 prisoners were loaded onto trucks and driven out of camp to the edge of the jungle overlooking the flat land that stretched for some distance down the beach on the eastern shore of the Sulu Sea. The prisoners were lined up in formation as the prison camp commander, Captain Kishamoto, took spade in hand and formally broke ground for the project. Mac thought the guards were crazy when they threw their arms in the air, yelled and shouted approval. Roy Henderson figured it would be a road to nowhere, and whispered to Mac and Smitty, "This sure is a strange place to start building a road." Just as puzzled, Mac whispered, "You can say that again. I can't figure out why they'd want a road built out here." One good look at the area convinced them it was no road-building project, which is what the prisoners had been told when they were aboard the ship. For the next two years, the 300 men of POW camp Palawan Barracks would spend their working hours building an airstrip for the Japanese Air Force. When completed it would be the second largest airfield in the Philippines.

It was exhausting work. They had no heavy equipment, no bulldozers, no earth-moving equipment or trucks to haul away the dirt and debris. Instead, they relied on picks, shovels, one axe for each group of men, wheelbarrows, and what energy each man could muster for the workday.

The completed Palawan airfield, before the bombings, with its concrete runway down the center and two dirt runways. There were concrete turnoffs for the Japanese Zeros stationed there (U.S. War Department).

With the one ax, the men took turns hacking away at the coconut and palm trees in the path of the landing strip. They worked hard most of the time, knowing that if they took a break, goofed off or didn't carry the required load, they'd be beaten to the ground by the guards. The guards used a short club, a bit thicker than an officer's woven leather "swagger stick" or riding crop. These short clubs could inflict a lot of pain, especially when applied to the kidneys or the back of the head. A guard who knew how to use the club could drop a man to his knees with one blow. The work crew guards were changed daily, but the treatment was always the same, except on days when Smiley watched over them. Otherwise, the club came down swiftly and often on the head and back of any prisoner who even appeared to be goofing off. That's why all the prisoners wanted Smiley to guard them. They dreaded even the sight of the guards they had nicknamed "The Bull," "Puss 'n' Boots" and "High Pockets." These three were experts at inflicting pain without breaking the bones of the prisoners, who they knew were needed for the almost impossible job of building an airfield by hand. The meanest, most brutal guards were either former front-line troops immersed in the culture of Bushido, or the misfits of the Japanese Army who felt beating and killing prisoners increased their worth.

They were getting into the routine: Up in the morning for the flag raising and exercises, their mess kit of rice, then to the airfield for another day of hard work under an unforgiving Philippine sun. In the early stages, the workday consisted of at least ten hours of work, six days a week. They had Sundays off. On days when a welcome rainstorm hit the island, they'd stay in the barracks talking about home. When Mac started his day in the field, he worked with Smitty, Roy, Evan Bunn and Clarence Clough. Bunn and Clough slept next to them. They had a lot in common, and it wasn't long before the five had bonded. After long conversations with Bunn and Clough in the barracks and working with them in the field, Mac, Smitty and Roy thought they were good, trustworthy guys and invited them into their survival group. They all agreed they could survive Palawan with each other's help.

They'd been on the island only eleven days when the first prison break occurred. It was August 11, 1942, when six men made their escape. The barbed wire which surrounded the camp hadn't been put in place yet when three Marines and three sailors made their escape by running from the camp in the dead of night. Of the six, Marine Buddy Henderson was shot and killed in Aborlan, a small village south of Puerto Princesa, by two Filipinos who had sided with the Japanese. Another Filipino at Palawan got word to the POWs that Marine Sydney Wright killed the two Filipinos before he and the other escapees made good on their flight into the jungle. There was no word on how Wright had killed the Filipinos, and the Palawan prisoners heard no more about the other escapees: C.W. Davis, 4th Marines; R.W. Keeland, Bruce Elliott, and K.M. Hodges, all U.S. Navy. Navy Seaman Bruce Elliott, now a retired Navy Boatswain's Mate living in Garden Grove, California, later said the six of them escaped over a wall.

The local priest had provided Elliott with an alarm clock, a compass and a small map of the Philippines for navigation. Elliott then talked the five other men into making the break with him. The escapees, led by Elliott, stole a native barco. They used the alarm clock for tacking, swinging the leaky little boat to the left (port side) for 15 minutes, and then tacking to the right (starboard) for the same period, but always moving south. They set a tattered sail and made their way to Brookes Point in southern Palawan, where they joined Filipino guerrillas. They spent much of the rest of the war with Filipino guerrillas (Moros), attacking Japanese outposts, not only on Palawan, but also on other islands in the Philippine chain, killing Japanese and blowing up oil tanks. It wasn't until March of 1944 that Elliott and the others were picked up by a sub, the USS Narwhal,

which took them to Australia. Officers at MacArthur's headquarters said
they were probably the first POWs to escape from an established POW
camp. Throughout the war, only a handful, maybe 20 to 25 prisoners, were
able to escape from their Japanese captors in the Philippines.

The camp commandant, Captain Kishamoto, was angry. Having never
faced the problem of a prison escape before, he asked higher-ups in Manila
what penalties he should hand out. As a result, all the prisoners received
one-third rations, or one mess kit of rice per day for three days; their
movements were restricted to the barbed wire enclosure, and armed guards
patrolled inside as well as outside the camp day and night. As a result, no
work was done on the airfield, and the hungry inhabitants of Palawan Barracks were left dreaming and talking about food—their favorite dishes, who
cooked them, and how they were prepared. As a civilian Mac had had pancakes, prepared by his sisters or his mother, every morning before heading off to school or work. He loved pancakes, remembering that on the
day he left for boot camp, his sisters were up and about earlier than usual,
preparing his last pancake breakfast as a civilian. But now, he was overwhelmed by the desire for one dessert food he couldn't get off his mind.
During the long months when his stomach screamed for food, he could
think of only one dessert: an angel food cake with a hole carved out of the
middle to make room for a huge glob of ice cream. He lusted for that cake
and ice cream almost every day he was on the island. The prisoners never
stopped searching for food, and whenever they had the chance, Mac and
his buddies would forage in the jungle for fruit or for anything that
crawled, slithered, walked or flew—snakes, lizards, monkeys or birds. It
was all considered edible.

After the three-day lockdown ended, it was back to work, and after
the morning ceremony—flag raising, calisthenics and rice—the prisoners
were trucked to the airfield and put to work busting coral and hauling
debris to the shoreline. The weather always cooperated, or seemed to, and
there were very few days spent sitting in the barracks waiting for a storm
to end. The northeast side of Palawan, where Puerto Princesa was located,
did not get as much rain as the western side, or the eastern side farther to
the south. All the while, the daily labor was slowly taking its toll on the
prisoners. As they labored away at the airfield, the heat and meager rice
diet combined to take away the pounds from the already frail bodies of
the men who had fought the good fight at Bataan and Corregidor and
who in the final days of the battle had had little to eat before they became
prisoners of war. If they worked hard on the airstrip, they worked just as
hard looking for something to eat. The Japanese guards established a set
of rules: As long as you found the food—bananas, papayas, coconuts,
lizards, snakes, even monkeys and some birds—you could eat it, but it had

to be eaten at the job site and not carried into the prison. Anyone caught carrying food through the front gate would be beaten to the ground. Naturally, both guards and prisoners called it "forbidden fruit."

Mac would eat anything put before him, with one exception—monkey. He just couldn't do it. To the Iowa boy, the sight of a monkey roasting on a spit looked too much like a human baby. However, he thought roasted snake was delicious: "Tastes just like chicken," he told the others. There were a lot of snakes on Palawan, but the snake collectors had to be very careful. It wasn't at all uncommon to come face to face with a cobra, one of the deadliest snakes in the world and quite common in the rain forests of Palawan. Poisonous? Yes, but Mac thought they were good eating, too.

Heraclio Arispe, from Corpus Christi, Texas, slept next to Mac, although not under the same mosquito netting. It was late at night when Arispe woke everyone in the barracks as he screamed and ran around the room like a crazed animal. It was difficult for Mac or anyone else to understand what he was trying to say. When his words finally got through to the others in the hut, they all looked to the floor and saw what Arispe was screaming about. A huge ten-foot python had somehow found an opening in the barracks and slithered in and across the sleeping Arispe. The luckless python was killed that night, and all the POWs who ate it thought the big snake was delicious.

"Boots" was an odd sort of guy. At least, that's what Mac and the others thought. He wore a pair of black, shiny boots, never communicated much with the other prisoners and spent his spare time in the prison picking up as much of the Japanese language as he could. He would sit off to one side and practice writing the Japanese alphabet and speaking the language he'd picked up from the guards. The other prisoners, Mac included, hated Boots. He was chummy with the guards, and he'd taken an avid interest in Japanese culture.

Shortly after the first escape, Mac watched as Boots walked up to a guard, asked for and received some paper and a pencil. He hurriedly scribbled a note and then tucked it away in his boot. Mac and Smitty figured he was up to something. He was just too sneaky for them, and they always kept watch on him while they worked at shoveling and busting coral. One day they heard Boots getting permission to relieve himself. When he walked into the jungle, Mac and Smitty followed him. Out of sight of the guards, the two grabbed Boots and went to work on him. Mac looked at him as the temper he'd been trying to control rose to the surface. "Where's the note, Boots? Give us the note. You tryin' to hide something?" Both Mac and Smitty jabbed at Boots, backing him up even deeper into the jungle. "Leave me alone, just leave me alone!" he whined. "I'll start yelling if you don't get away and leave me alone!" Boots started yelling, and Mac who now hated the sight of him, pushed him to the ground and put his foot on Boots' throat, telling Smitty to grab the note. The note was written in Japanese, and although neither Mac nor Smitty could read it, they figured someone in the camp would be able to translate it.

Leaving Boots huddled in the bushes, too frightened to come out, the two Marines walked out of the jungle and went back to work. Back at Palawan Barracks that evening, they found one man among the 300 prisoners in the camp who could read a little Japanese. It was a rough translation, but they all got the message. Boots addressed the note to Captain Kishamoto, asking that he be allowed to join the Japanese Army. He would, he said, be giving up his American citizenship. What happened next was predictable. Someone in the crowd yelled, "That dirty bastard, I'll kill him!" "If I don't get to him first!" Mac yelled back. The men stormed out of the barracks looking for the traitor. They found him huddled in the corner of the courtyard, shaking like a leaf. There were screams of, "You're a dead man, Boots!" and "You're gonna' hang, ya' goddamn traitor!" Someone got some rope and threw one end over a tree limb. A couple prisoners grabbed Boots and started pushing him toward the tree while Boots kept yelling and screaming for help. His cries for help were in Japanese and that alerted the guards, who came running into the prison.

Captain Kishamoto also heard the commotion. He walked into the prison yard as the guards pounded on the prisoners, yelling at them to break it up. After some more pounding, the prisoners gave up and released Boots. Captain Kishamoto wanted to know what was going on, and one of the prisoners told him about the note and its contents. Surprisingly, the prison camp commander wasn't pleased. He ordered Boots locked up in the prison jail. Soon after the incident Boots was sent back to Manila. The day Boots left Palawan Barracks, Kishamoto was heard to say, "Anyone who turns against his own country deserves to be killed!"

On August 29, 1942, Palawan Barracks experienced its second prison break. Two sailors, Charles Watkins and Joe Paul, took a break from working on the airstrip and, with the guard's permission, walked into the jungle to relieve themselves. The Japanese never saw them again. They made a clean break and were led out of the area by a Filipino guide. The other prisoners learned of the successful escape from Filipino men who crept close enough to the airfield work site to tell them what had happened.

There were the expected repercussions. Once the break was discovered, the prisoners were hauled back to camp from the airfield and spent three days confined to their barracks. Again, they received only one mess kit of rice a day. But there was more. This time the POWs were divided into groups of 10, and each man was given a number. If there were any more escapes, Mac knew there would be hell to pay. Each 10-man group would have its own guard, and again it was a begging contest to see which group could get Smiley. Mac's group wasn't always successful at this. The brutal treatment of the other guards made life on Palawan Island a little tougher each day.

The Japanese Army had 300 prisoner of war camps stretching throughout Asia during World War II. There were camps in China, Manchuria, Burma, Formosa, Japan, French Indochina, Korea, the Philippines, Sumatra and Thailand. Thousands of prisoners were crammed into these camps, and most were put to work as slave laborers. Some were needed to work the mines, delivering the raw materials necessary to keep Japan's war machine running. Thus, the prisoners, like the Americans at Puerto Princesa's Palawan Barracks, were not to be killed, but kept alive — kept alive at least long enough to produce for the Japanese Empire.

If the guards couldn't kill the prisoners, at least they could brutalize them. The number of beatings increased daily. Meanwhile, Mac was rather proud of himself. He hadn't had a temper flare-up for some time, and he thought he was beginning to control himself. But one day, as he was helping cut down a coconut tree, a guard started jabbering at him. Mac didn't know what he was saying; he couldn't understand very many words of Japanese yet. Mac thought he'd be cooperative. He said, "Okay." He didn't see the club coming towards his face. The guard's club hit him squarely in the mouth, and it sent him reeling back and to the ground. As he lay there with a bloody mouth and a loose tooth, he felt fortunate. He'd watched beatings of other prisoners that were much worse, and he thought to himself he was starting to control his temper. Difficult to do, he admitted, but at least he was controlling it and surviving.

Mac was working on the airfield with Smitty and Henderson, and Smitty was giving Mac his weekly lecture on temper control and work ethics. Mac was goofing off, and did nothing more than pick up a half-shovel of dirt at a time. "Mac! Damnit! They're goin' to bust you in the head again if you don't start working a little harder! Mac just smiled, and looked up just in time to see the guard whack Smitty on the head. This put a crease in Smitty's pith helmet, and the blow put the tall Texas down on one knee. Mac couldn't help but giggle as Smitty stood up and went back to work. It wouldn't be the last time Mac heard Smitty's lectures on working hard to stay alive, and all three would be hit on the head time after time during the months they were on Palawan. The blows to the head would have a more serious effect on Roy Henderson toward the end of their imprisonment at Puerto Princesa.

Army Sergeant Levi Mullins was a nice guy. Bullheaded, but nice. In early October of '42, he got into an argument about the war with one of the guards. The Japanese guard said American forces in the Pacific were defeated. Mullins didn't agree and, despite the guard's insistence, would not admit to an American defeat. The guard was furious. He picked up a club and swung it at Mullins' head. Mullins would have been brained on the spot had it hit its intended target. But Mullins raised his arm in defense and the club broke his arm. The next day Mullins was trucked to work with a sling on his arm, and worked all day using only one arm. The same guard engaged him again in an argument over who was winning the war, but still Mullins would not back down. This time, the guard walked away.

The Japanese had a special hatred for the United States Marines, a hatred which would be played out tragically on scores of battlefields during the Pacific War. In the early days of the war, Japanese soldiers would ask a prisoner whether he was Army, Navy or Marine. If he answered, "Marine," or, the Japanese translation, "Rikusentai," he stood a chance of receiving harsher treatment than other prisoners. Some of the Japanese soldiers thought that, in order to become a Marine, a recruit had to kill either his mother or father. Some of the Marine POWs were asked which one they killed. Most of the Marines who were asked didn't hesitate to give them an answer—either mom or dad—which seemed to satisfy the guards.

By this time, almost all the prisoners in Palawan Barracks had formed into small groups of three to five men. Tropical diseases, the lack of a proper diet, malaria and other illnesses were taking a toll among the prisoners. The smaller groups provided some assurance of help or moral support—food when needed, maybe some help in making a pair of shorts or making shoes out of old slats. And if a member became sick, others in his group would be able to eat the sick prisoner's food rather than letting it go to waste. Pacts were made, and there was general agreement within each group, including Mac's buddies, Smitty, Roy, Clough and Bunn, that they would take care of each other. "We will not let the Japs win in our camp!" they all agreed. Buoyed by each other's support, some of the "salty" attitude so common among U.S. servicemen who had fought at Bataan and Corregidor, returned to help lift their spirits.

5

Guerrilla Contact

J.O. Warren, the camp's barber, didn't have much in the way of shaving equipment to work with when Smitty got in trouble. Smitty was "goosey," and when a man is afflicted with that incurable condition, he will sooner or later get in trouble, whether he wants to or not. It was just outside the barracks. where they gathered after a hard day's labor at the airfield when a prisoner, no one knew who, gleefully suggested to one of the guards that if he wanted to see a man jump, really jump, he should sneak up behind ol' Smitty and give him a goose. The guard sneaked up behind Smitty and shoved his hand into the lower portion of Smitty's backside. Smitty, who had grown a full beard, automatically responded with a quick jump into the air. On his way down, he got very angry. He landed and made a quick turnaround. As Smitty spun, his fist came with him, and it landed squarely on the guard's jaw, knocking him unconscious. The guard fell to the ground. Nothing funny about it. Smitty could have been beaten, tortured or killed for what he had just done. Several men grabbed him and hustled him to the barracks to hide him from the guard, who was just coming around. Fast work by Warren probably saved Smitty's life, or at least spared him from great bodily injury. Warren's original homemade razor was nowhere to be found, but he was one of the few prisoners who was still wearing his service shoes. He tore one of the shoes apart, pulled the metal arch support out of it and then honed a sharp edge by grinding it on a rock. Not quite a razor, but it would do, and Warren gave Smitty a painful but effective dry shave. They thought barber Warren was a hell of a guy.

With his heavy beard removed, Smitty's face was as white and tender as a baby's butt. He needed camouflaging. Some of the prisoners took dirt, spit into it to make mud and smeared it across his face. Then they hid him. When the guards came looking for Smitty, they couldn't find him. He wasn't out of the woods yet. The camp's doctor, Carl Mango, kept Smitty on sick call for about ten days, hoping the guard would forget what he looked like. The offended guard waited every morning at the camp gate, his bayonet fixed on his rifle, looking for Smitty in the column of prisoners headed for work on the airfield runway. He wasn't among them. Smitty was under the protection of the wonderful camp doctor, Carl Mango.

The Doc had other talents he'd honed as a young man. Mango told one young prisoner who was trying to pick a fight to settle down. The prisoner looked at Mango and asked if he wanted "to make something out of it." Dr. Mango said, "Why not?" The prisoner moved in quickly, but before he could take a swing, he was knocked flat by a hard right to the head. The prisoner looked up from the dirt, saw Mango standing over him, and got up. Both men shook hands and agreed there would be no hard feelings. Doc Mango was as quick with his fists as he was with his scalpel.

Some prisoners panic at any hint of punishment, and one of those prisoners, considered a real "stoolie" by some, said he was going to tell the prison officers that Smitty was the one who had knocked out the guard. He feared that if someone didn't rat on Smitty, all of them would be punished. Theodore McNally from Joplin, Missouri, wasn't having any of that. He took a small knife from his mess kit, walked over to the stoolie, grabbed him by the throat, put the knife to his jugular vein and said, "I'll kill you right here, you son of a bitch, if you say one word. And if they ever find out it was Smitty, I'll suspect it was you that told, and I'll kill ya' even if you say you didn't tell. Understand me, asshole?" McNally pushed him so hard he stumbled backward across the floor, hitting the wall on the other side of the barracks. Eventually, the guard gave up looking for his assailant, and life returned to near-normal at Palawan Barracks.

Slacking Off

The prisoners were learning to pace themselves. They managed to slow their work pace without angering the guards and feeling the impact of a club on the head. The meager rice diet and the daily labor forced them to slow down. But some prisoners went a little too far. Mac was one of them. He wasn't going to give the guards any more work than he had to, and that was that. He would pick up less than a shovel full of dirt, stand there looking around … then he'd toss the dirt. He'd look around a while longer and then put his spade back into the ground, where he would pick up a small amount of dirt, shake some of it off the shovel, and toss the rest of it back on the ground. In short, he wasn't doing any work at all, and this was beginning to anger Smitty, who said, "Dole, you lazy rascal, you're gonna get us all in trouble. Don't you realize you're makin' it harder on yourself by goin' so doggone slow?" Mac showed his stubbornness, saying, "I don't give a damn if it is harder on me, Smitty, they're not gonna get any more work out of me than I want them to." With that, he pitched another small amount of dirt back on the ground.

Smitty spotted the guard first and yelled to Mac, "One of them rascals is comin' toward ya, Dole, and you're gonna get cracked. He's madder than a hornet!" It was Mac who stopped what little he was doing and yelled at Smitty, "Go ahead, let the son of a bitch hit me. I don't give a damn!" The guard obliged. He came up from behind and cracked him on the head, his pith helmet provided little protection from the club. The blow dropped Mac to his knees. He got up slowly, looked the guard right in the eyes and yelled, "Ya' didn't hurt me, you son of a bitch." He realized the moment he'd called the guard a son of a bitch that it was a stupid reply. The guard replied with another clubbing, this one even worse, to the side of the head. Mac went all the way down this time. He lay there, his face flushing red with anger, then slowly got to his feet, brushing himself off. Again, he looked the Jap in the eyes and yelled, "Ya still didn't hurt me, you son of a bitch!" The guard looked puzzled. He shook his head, said, "Ya baka!" ("You're crazy!") and walked off. Smitty shook his head. Squinting from the bright sun, he yelled at his buddy, "You are stupid, Dole. He could have killed you. Quit pushing your luck!" Mac grinned at Smitty and said, "Well, he didn't kill me, did he?"

They went back to work, but it wasn't long before "Dole" was back to his old tricks. He would have been called a "slacker" back home, but he wasn't about to contribute any more than necessary to the Japanese war effort. Smitty, was concerned about all the beatings Mac had taken and pushed him aside to do some of his work. Mac just stood there watching and grinning as the tall Texan shoveled while he rested his arms on his shovel. The guards became more impatient with him, and Mac lost count of how many times he was beaten to the ground. His pith helmet had a huge crease down the middle from all the beatings he'd taken. How many times had he heard Smitty admonishing him, "You're gonna get yourself killed one of these days, Dole."

Another incident increased his hatred of the Japanese even more. He found his Urbandale High School class ring and then lost it to a Japanese guard. He'd returned to the barracks after a long day of labor at the airstrip and was placing his blanket on the floor when he noticed something shiny wedged between the floorboards. He could hardly believe what he pulled from the floor—his high school class ring! He had thought he'd lost it for good. A big smile crossed his face as he placed it on his finger. When he got up the next morning for another day in the field, he forgot about the ring being on his finger, and when he got to the work site, a guard spotted it right away. The guard wasted no time. He ran over to Mac and told him to take the ring off his finger. Mac did everything he could to keep the ring, twisting and pulling on it and telling the guard it wouldn't come off his hand. It didn't work. The guard looked at Mac, smiled and said, "I cut your finger off then!" He pulled his bayonet out of its scabbard. Mac had no choice and handed the ring to the guard. More angry at himself than at anyone else, he explained to an understanding Smitty, "How could I have been so stupid to forget I had it on?" Smitty just looked at him and didn't answer. They both went back to work.

With his high school class ring now on the finger of a Japanese guard, the only item left among his personal possessions that reminded him of home was his bible, but that would soon turn up missing. It had been given to him by one of his Urbandale High School teachers, Miss Lela B. Stevens. She taught history, and it was one of Mac's least favorite subjects. To make matters worse, the student and his teacher didn't get along. Miss Stevens had made every effort to get through to him. It was on his last day at school, before heading to Marine boot camp in San Diego, that the history teacher had stopped him in the hallway and said, "Glenn, I know we haven't seen eye-to-eye on a lot of things, but I want to give you this bible to take with you when you leave." Glenn thanked Miss Stevens and walked out of the school with the bible in hand. He'd carried it with him and had read it from time to time during the past two years. With the loss of his class ring and bible, he had lost the only two worldly possessions that reminded him of home. But he could still dream of home.

Contact Beyond the Barbed Wire

In October of '42, the Japanese brought in about 100 replacements for the prisoners of Palawan who'd been felled by malaria and dengue fever. The sick had been taken from the island and returned to Manila, where they were said to have received some treatment for the illness, whatever that might have been. The Japanese did not provide quinine and other medicines to the sick prisoners of Palawan, and with completion of the airstrip a top priority, the POWs were working longer hours. Work on Sundays was becoming part of their regular schedule.

The first time it happened, he was nearly scared out of his wits. When a prisoner had to relieve himself, he usually was given permission by a guard to step into the jungle and away from the work site. It happened shortly after their arrival on Palawan. Work was progressing at the airstrip. Given permission to relieve himself, Mac headed into the darkness of the jungle. As he stood there out of the sun and away from the sound of metal on coral and the haranguing of the guards, a voice said, "Hey Joe! Don't look! I leave something for you!" When he heard someone running deeper into the jungle, he turned to look in the direction of the voice. No one there, but the Filipino who'd taken the risk of contacting a prisoner had left a piece of bread on a coral rock. Other prisoners Mac talked to reported they, too, had made secret contact with Filipinos, who roamed through the heavy cover and out of sight of the Japanese guards. Contact had been made and, in addition to an occasional gift of food, the Filipinos passed on what little information they'd received on what was happening in the world beyond Palawan. It wasn't much.

Although they had no idea of what was happening elsewhere in the Pacific, they would have shouted for joy had they have known that in a two-day sea battle in early June of '42, the U.S. had scored a decisive victory in the Battle of Midway. In August of '42, the first U.S. amphibious landing of the war occurred when the 1st Marine Division invaded Tulagi and Guadalcanal in the Solomon Islands. The Japanese were just beginning to experience defeat. Up to that time there had been little for Americans to cheer about. There were no cheers coming from Palawan, because the prisoners didn't know of events underway beyond the prison camp and the airfield, but the war was drawing closer to them and their island.

With what little free time they had at the end of the day, they sat around and listened to each other's stories, stories they'd heard time and time again, anything to break the boredom. Had he have been back in the states, Mac could have walked through Smitty's home in Hughes Springs, Texas, blindfolded and wouldn't even have knocked over a lamp. Mac knew Smitty's house inside and out, and could even tell you the wallpaper patterns in the various rooms and the color of the curtains. Of course, Smitty and Roy could have described Mac's house and his trailer bedroom. They would have recognized his mother, dad, sisters and brothers at first glance. That's how detailed their discussions were—anything to break the boredom and get their minds off their life in a prison camp.

Mac loved to tell about his family's homestead in far western Nebraska, where they had lived when he was a kid. It had been 160 acres near Melbeta, just southeast of Scottsbluff. The country was in the midst of the Great Depression and, as Mac remembered it, it was a time of drought, dust and grasshoppers—millions of grasshoppers. So many insects that there was always the crunching sound of feet on locusts. Only

40 acres were tillable, and that was in wheat. The other 120 acres helped maintain some cattle, a few hogs and chickens. Mac's dad, David, was on the road most of the time looking for work. His mother, Dessa, delegated the chores and watched over her children. Mac remembers her garden. She had a knack for making things grow, and a lot of what they ate came out of Dessa's garden. It was a beautiful garden, he would tell his buddies.

As brutal and boring and isolated as their life was, there was still some contact with the outside world. Not much, but some, and that was about to be cut off. It was in December of '42, the year and month that Enrico Fermi conducted the world's first nuclear chain reaction, which paved the way for the first nuclear bomb.

The Japanese discovered some American prisoners were making contact with the Filipinos while working on the airfield. They learned that the Filipinos were not only giving them news, but food as well. The passing of information and the food drop-off center was an old abandoned shack near the work site. The prisoners had taken an empty can and placed notes, sometimes money, if there was any money available, into the can. A Filipino sneaked into the shack each day and left food or information. This went on for some time until one day the Filipino left a note telling the prisoners the Japanese were watching him and he wouldn't be able to help them any longer. He feared for his life and the lives of his family. One of the prisoners, Jimmy Barna, wanted more information and left another note asking for information about the Japanese garrison on the island—how many soldiers there were, where were they located and any other information concerning the garrison. Japanese guards found the note in the shack and, as Mac later said, "All hell broke loose."

The Japanese located the Filipino and brought him to the prison camp. They told all the Palawan POWs to line up in formation. They marched the Filipino man and his young son up and down the lines at gun point. The Filipino pointed out two prisoners who had been communicating with him. Barna and the other prisoner were pulled out of the ranks. Guards entered the barracks and started searching for cans of corned beef, which they said had been stolen from a prison storeroom. Mac and the others watched as guards came running from the barracks holding up cans of corned beef. They claimed that the cans had been found among the personal possessions of four other inmates, and they were pulled from the ranks and joined the other prisoners in the camp's jail.

Captain Kishamoto ordered beatings for all six prisoners. Again, the POWs were called out of their barracks. All work details ceased, and all the prisoners lined up in formation to witness the beatings. Kishamoto ordered two guards, Tomioko, called "The Bull" by the prisoners, and another brute, Manichi Nishitoni, the camp's head cook, to administer

The coconut trees which lined the path inside Palwan Barracks, Camp 10A. Rufus Smith would shinny up the trees at night to steal coconuts. The trees were also the site of prisoner beatings. As the camp's inmates stood in formation, the prisoners who were being punished were told to wrap their arms around the trunks of the trees. They would then be whipped and clubbed (U.S. War Department).

the beatings. Mac stood there gritting his teeth. He could tell the two men enjoyed their assignment. It was brutal. Their first beating victim was a muscular, well-built Marine named Jack Taylor. Taylor took pride in his body and worked out on homemade barbells and lifted heavy rocks to keep in shape, despite the fact he was losing weight as fast as the other POWs. Taylor stood against one of the coconut trees in the courtyard. They didn't tie him to the tree, but made him face it and put his arms around the trunk. Mac believed the Japanese were hoping Taylor would make a run for it, but he didn't. Tomioko and Nishitoni went about their work. Nishitoni smiled as he ordered one of the other guards to beat Taylor across the small of the back with a small wire whip. It tore into his flesh, ripping his skin away from the bone. When the guard tired, Nishitoni ordered still another guard to take his turn. Slowly, they turned Taylor's backside into raw, bleeding meat. Still another guard was ordered to beat him again, and this time with a large pole, which he applied to Taylor's shoulders, the back of his head, his back, shoulders and butt.

When they finished with Taylor they moved on to the next prisoner, who received the same treatment. When a guard became so tired he could not lift his arms he was replaced with still another guard, and if Nishitoni didn't think the beatings were strong enough, he'd take the whip or club from the guard and continue the beating himself. The guards seemed to enjoy the beatings. They laughed as the whips and clubs smashed into raw, shredded flesh. As for the victims, most of them stood there, heads unbowed and making no sound as they were beaten. If they passed out during the beating, water was thrown on them to revive them and the beating continued. One of the victims, a Marine named Yoder, a former boxer, passed out. When the water was thrown in his face, he stood up and went into a fight stance. He'd been beaten so badly, he'd forgotten where he was. The other POWs yelled at Yoder, letting him know he wasn't in the ring. Fortunately, Yoder's mind cleared, and he put up no resistance as they beat him.

When the beatings ended, guards dragged the six men to the brig, where Tomioko beat each man about the face until they were unconscious. They were then dragged inside and thrown into a cell, where they were put on a diet of a half a mess kit of rice every three days. Mac and the others had to walk past the beaten prisoners every day as they headed out to work on the airfield. As they passed, the six prisoners raised their shirts to show the extent of their injuries—massive black and blue areas on their bodies. They weren't in the prison much longer. All six were shipped back to Manila. When their replacements arrived on Palawan, they said that Marine Jimmy Barna, who wrote the notes to the Filipinos, and a sailor identified only as Laidlaw, were supposed to have been executed. They had heard that the four other prisoners, including weight lifter Jack Taylor, had been sent to Bilibid Prison.

Shortly after these beatings, Captain Kishamoto ordered the prisoners to put the camp into top shape. They spent an entire day cleaning up the barracks and courtyard. The captain issued blue denim trousers and shirts to each prisoner, who by now wore tattered dungarees, homemade shorts or jock straps. They were allowed to take showers and shave for the big inspection. The POWs were lucky to get a bath a week, and that usually occurred on their return from work when guards took small groups down to the ocean and let them swim. What Mac and the prisoners didn't know at the time was that they would be inspected by members of the International Red Cross. On the day the Red Cross entered the camp, the prisoners stood at attention in the courtyard while the inspectors checked their barracks and then continued the inspection by walking up and down the rows of prisoners, hardly pausing to look closely at them. No prisoner was allowed to talk to the inspectors, nor were the inspectors allowed to talk to them. The whole thing took only about a half-hour, and then the inspectors walked out of the gate without so much as a look back. No sooner had the gate closed than guards rushed into the barracks and forced the men to return the denim trousers and shirts. When they discovered that it had been a Red Cross inspection, they complained it was all a hoax to trick the Red Cross into thinking everything was fine. And as far as the Mac was concerned the Red Cross really didn't care. He would say later, "The inspectors could tell we suffered from malnutrition, but nothing came of it. They made their half-hour inspection, and that's all they cared about."

The prisoners were bored. If they weren't working on the airstrip, there was nothing to do but sit in the barracks and talk. Smitty was the first one to break out of the doldrums as he lay on his back in the barracks. It had been another long, exhausting day at the airfield. He raised his head, looked at Mac and said, "Sure wish we could get a poker game goin'." "Poker?" said Mac, "How in hell are we gonna play poker?" Just then, a little light came on in the Iowa boy's head. He thought about all those vitamin boxes he'd saved. Even though vitamins were no longer given to them—a short-lived, phony attempt at showing some concern for the starving prisoners—Mac still had about a hundred of the empty vitamin boxes. The cardboard boxes, if cut and marked properly, could be made into a deck of cards. Crude as that might be, they would work. All he needed was some way of numbering and marking the individual cards. The solution came the next morning.

As they marched into Puerto Princesa to their trucks, which would take them to the air field, Mac raised his hand, a signal to the Jap guards that he needed a "benjo," or a "piss call," as American GIs would put it. The column stopped. Mac, along with some other prisoners, including Smitty, ran directly into the old abandoned schoolhouse in the town. With Smitty acting as a lookout, he worked fast. Running from room to room in the deserted building, Mac looked for anything that might help him build a deck of cards. His scavenging paid off. As if the long-gone teacher had left them for him, he found three pens, one black, one blue and one red, lying side by side on a desk. He was in business. Shoving the pens into his pocket, he rejoined the column and marched off to work.

It didn't take much to excite someone who suffered from day-to-day boredom. Smitty was on him right away with, "Did ya' find any Dole? Did ya' find anything at all?" With a big grin on his face, Mac said, "Tell everybody there's going to be a poker game tomorrow night." Smitty jumped with joy. "Oh, hot dog, Dole! I can feel the old cards in my hands already."

He paused just a second in thought and then said, "Hey, by the way, don't you think since we're responsible for this we should get a percentage of the games?" Mac grinned again. "You bet I do, my friend! You bet I do!"

Mac could hardly wait for the workday to end. He was so excited about getting back to the barracks to work on the cards that he actually did a little work at the field. When they returned to the prison at the end of the day, he hurriedly washed and ate, then went to work designing the cards. The finished product looked pretty good, and it could well be that his ability to draw and design came from helping his father, a sign painter back in Iowa. "If I might say so," Mac said, "these ol' cards look pretty good." An excited Smitty couldn't have been more pleased at the outcome, saying, "You betcha, Dole, they are great!" Mac had spent hours designing the cards. Diamonds, hearts, spades and clubs were all carefully drawn. He drew the Jokers to look like the guards, and the Kings were all U.S. Marines. They played poker that night, and the card-making paid off. When they took their "percentage" off the top of all the gambling proceeds, Smitty had all the cigarettes he needed for a long time, and Mac, the non-smoker, came out of it with what he wanted most, extra food. He was hungry, always hungry.

If anything was constant at the Palawan prison camp, it was hunger. When he had the time to think of home, food was always a part of the daydream. Life hadn't been easy for millions of Americans in the late '30s, and Mac's family didn't have a lot of money. Food for the table had been scarce at times. There were days when the diet was potatoes and milk, supplemented at times with a little bread. But this was Palawan, where gnawing hunger was a constant companion. If you were lucky enough to trap a python, cobra, lizard or monkey, they were eaten right away—even rotten fish heads were added to the pot when available.

February 1943

In February, 1943, when the Japanese began evacuating Guadalcanal after a long and costly fight with the 1st Marine Division, there was, miles away, another "hell to pay" event on Palawan. The three buddies from the Cavite Navy Yard, Mac, Smitty and Roy, had been imprisoned at Puerto Princesa for six months when four more prisoners escaped from Palawan Barracks. They slipped out the back way through the barbed wire sometime during the night and made it down to the beach. Their tracks indicated they had slipped into a coconut grove. Although the Palawan prisoners had been cut off from most of the information received from Filipinos, word got back that two prisoners had been captured and sent back to Manila. The third escapee, Navy machinist Robert Pryor, had been captured and beheaded, his head displayed in a little village in northern Palawan. The fourth escapee had disappeared in the jungle, and there was no word whether he survived.

There was always the threat of reprisal for prison escapes. By now, all prisoners were in groups of ten, and they counted off every morning for the Japanese guards. Although it hadn't occurred on Palawan, in other Japanese prison camps where prisoners had been formed into groups, if any prisoner escaped, the remaining prisoners in his group were executed. But the Japanese needed slave labor, and executions at Palawan would be counterproductive. The airfield had to be finished, so the punishment this time was a cut in the rice rations for several days. Even a full ration of rice was barely enough to keep the hard-working prisoners alive, and malnutrition became so bad that many prisoners suffered from thin skin. Their skin tore easily, and special care had to be taken, especially in the crotch and under the arms. If the skin tore or was cut, it inevitably lead to infection and huge ulcers, some of them so big the prisoners couldn't lower their arms to their sides. An ulcer infection in the crotch was even more painful and always immobilized a prisoner. Mac had his share of skin ulcers. His formed on his butt and legs but they didn't slow him down. Lacking salt, he rubbed seawater into the sores. As painful as it was, the home remedy worked.

Rain was always welcome. If they were in the barracks and the rain started falling, they'd rush outside and stand there letting the rain wash all the salt and grime from their bodies. Then they sat around afterwards and talked about how nice a real shower with a large bar of soap would feel, then a good clean shave to get rid of the straggly beards almost all of them had and, finally, a dash of Old Spice shaving lotion. "Ah, the luxuries people in the U.S. have and don't realize it," they would say, and then the talk would move on to all the other creature comforts they'd had at home, a home so far away and so removed from the miserable life they led on Palawan Island.

Raymond Seagraves was from Lewisville, Texas. He was a big man, and he had lost a lot of weight because of the meager ration of rice and the hard work. His skin hung on him like a living blanket. Mac stood in awe when Seagraves would pull the skin away from his stomach and then knead it like bread dough. Japanese guards watching his performance called him "Baka" (Crazy). The prisoners called him, "Rubber."

At this point, Mac was still in fairly good shape, considering the circumstances. He'd lost some weight, had his share of body sores, and suffered a couple of bouts with malaria by that time. But he was not one of an increasing number of prisoners on Palawan who were flat on their backs suffering from diseases of hunger and the environment. Doc Mango had his hands full in the prison's hospital. Every day saw more prisoners lining up for whatever treatment was available; the number of prisoners too sick to work increased daily. All Mango had to work with was his black doctor's bag with the basic tools of a general practitioner of the 40s: A small supply of catgut for sewing up wounds, a scalpel, scissors, stethoscope, tweezers, thermometer and forceps. There was no medicine of any kind—no quinine, aspirin or any pain killing drugs. If a sick prisoner could no longer work, he was shipped back to Manila and healthier POWs were shipped in to replace him. To the Japanese, the airfield was a top priority, even if it took the lives of all the American POWs.

The prisoners sorely missed the entertainment that had been so much a part of their civilian lives: movies, plays, music and dancing. During one of their forays into the village under Japanese guard, they searched old buildings for anything they thought they could use. The guards weren't above doing a little foraging themselves. Clarence Clough ran across an old piano. He couldn't take the piano, couldn't even play one, but he tore out the piano wire, and in further foraging he found an old wood box. Clough took the box and the wire back to the barracks where he used a rock to hone the wire down to what he considered the right pitch. He strung the wire, five different strings in all, into a homemade banjo. He had a good voice, and so did Sergeant Doug Bogue. The two men entertained at night. They sang for hours. Entertainment fever hit the barracks, and it wasn't long before other prisoners joined in. One end of the barracks was cleared for their stage productions. They even had a stage curtain—nothing more than mosquito netting which was lowered between acts, but it worked. Showtime didn't last long, though. Fatigue and hunger wiped out any thoughts of Broadway.

Not only had the village's school building supplied Mac with the pens he needed to make a deck of cards, it also produced two basketball hoops and a bat and ball. If they didn't have to work on Sunday (the seven-day work week was becoming more frequent), they played basketball and baseball. That is, those prisoners who were healthy enough and had the energy to play. There weren't many of them, and before long all the game playing ended because of disease or fatigue. Meanwhile, efforts to complete construction of the airfield runway became more urgent. The three buddies, along with Evan Bunn and Clarence Clough, were laboring ten to twelve hours a day, and sometimes more, with Sundays considered a workday. There was no time left for anything but work and rest.

As if the Palawan prisoners hadn't had more than their share of beatings, an even more brutal guard appeared from time to time. If Mac and the other prisoners weren't dreaming about food, they dreamed about killing Taichi Deguchi. Deguchi was a Master Sergeant in the Imperial Army and was acting commander of the Palawan kempeitai, the army's military police and intelligence unit. Mac thought he was ten times worse than any other guard, and that included Nishitoni! He thought they were a lot alike, but Deguchi was meaner, handing out brutal beatings for even the smallest infractions. He beat prisoners for the fun of it, and Mac thought it was nothing more than a hobby for the son of a bitch. He was brutal and homicidal, and he was to be feared.

Clothing became a problem. Most prisoners had no shirts on their backs, and many of them were reduced to wearing nothing more than a homemade jockstrap. Mac, whose shoes had worn out some time ago, sported a pair of sandals cut from worn-out tires and far more comfortable, he thought, than the "clackers" which some prisoners wore. Clackers were made of wood, either from old doors or flooring found around Puerto Princesa. His dungarees had fallen apart from constant wear or jungle rot, or a combination of the two, and he replaced them by cutting up his old canvas sea bag and making a pair of shorts. He used his razor, a honed-down metal arch support from his old shoes, to do the cutting; then he shredded the canvas bag to get the necessary thread to sew the shorts together. He used an old piece of wire, honing down one end of it to a needlepoint sharpness to do the sewing. By now, his skin had been toughened to the sun, so he rarely wore his dungaree shirt, which was the only shirt he had.

6

An Unforeseen Threat

St. Patrick's Day, 1943

In early March, the U.S. declared a victory over the Japanese in the Battle of the Bismarck Sea. The Palawan POWs didn't hear about this, of course.

Mac opened his eyes slowly as the sun burned off the early morning haze and shone through the cracks in the barrack's roof. Something was wrong. He could feel it, and he reluctantly sat up and looked around as others in the barracks stumbled about, beginning their usual morning routine of dressing, running to the latrine, getting their rice ration before the morning formation and then heading off to the airfield for another day of hard labor.

He yawned, rubbed the sleep from his eyes and reached for his home-made rubber sandals. A sharp pain slashed across the lower right side of his body. It was so painful that all he could do was moan and grit his teeth. Smitty heard the moan and saw the expression on Mac's face. He leaned over, put his hand on his friend's shoulder and said, "What's wrong with ya', Dole?" Mac couldn't answer. Taking a couple of deep breaths he leaned to one side and braced himself with his left arm so he could keep the pressure off his right side. Slowly easing himself back on his blanket, he closed his eyes and brought his hand up to his forehead, placing his thumb on the left side of his temple, while he stretched his fingers across his face to cover the tears forming in his eyes. A horrible pain had engulfed him. He'd never been one to complain about pain, even when he'd had a severe bout with malaria, and he wasn't about to start now. But the pain was there. A lot of it, and it was hitting him so hard that beads of perspiration were forming on his face and chest. He knew Smitty was concerned about him, but whenever Mac felt pain, he just wanted to be left alone. Smitty sat quietly, remaining silent and looking at his buddy, ready to help in any way he could. Then the guards started yelling, ordering all the prisoners out of the barracks, screaming "Kuda! Kuda!" Mac knew that if he didn't get up and go to work he wouldn't get a full ration of rice. Smitty helped him up, and holding his side, which was burning with pain, Mac slipped on his sandals. Using Smitty as a brace, he put his hand on one knee and got up. Standing erect, the pain subsided just a bit as he walked out of the barracks, where angry guards complained about Mac's late arrival for morning formation.

They did their morning exercises, but Mac faked it. The pain in his side was intense. He and Smitty ate their ration of rice, and Smitty cleaned both mess kits before they headed off to the airfield. He grabbed his shovel, and using it as a crutch walked slowly to the work area, prodded and pushed along by the guards.

Although it was still early morning, the sun was beginning to bear down on Mac and the other POWs. The sun, coupled with pesky mosquitoes and flies, made Mac miserable. The sweat rolled down his back and legs as he toiled for several hours, never saying a word, while the only sounds were shovels cutting into the soil and scraping against the coral. His pain had turned into a dull ache, and as the day wore on it became more intense. He could hardly lift his leg to force the shovel into the ground. He lifted his arm to swat a fly and more pain shot through his body like an electric current, as if he'd just been bayoneted. A guard watching Mac ran over to him, yelling, "What wrong with you?" Mac gave a quick, angry reply, "I'm sick, you stupid son of a bitch!" The guard reaction was just as quick as he clubbed him on the head, dropping him to his knees. The guard yelled "Kuda! Kuda!" and Mac went back to work. As he worked, he couldn't help thinking that the language barrier between guards and prisoners was slowly breaking down. The guard definitely knew what a son of a bitch was.

By mid-afternoon the pain was so intense he could hardly move. He could no longer stand and fell to the ground. As he laid there, he felt his stomach and knew there was a lot of swelling. The whole stomach area was red and inflamed. They carried him back to the barracks. When they got there, Doc Mango was waiting at the front gate. Mango looked at him and gave a quick diagnosis: "Mac, I think it's your appendix and it's about to rupture. I'm afraid we're gonna have to operate, or you're not gonna make it." All the Iowa Marine could do was nod his head in approval.

Mango turned to the guards and told them what he'd have to do. Since there was no place for surgery at Palawan Barracks, the guards said they'd take Mac and the Doc to the Iwahig Penal Colony a few miles to the south, almost on the other side of the bay. Once they loaded him on the truck, they were off on a bumpy ride. It took at least an hour, on a road that was hardly more than a path for the water buffalo and the Filipinos who walked it. Smitty watched helplessly as the truck pulled away from the prison. Mac looked back to see Smitty standing in the road waving goodbye, while the guards pushed and prodded the Texan back into the prison. The ride seemed to take forever, with every bump absolute torture, and when he moaned in pain the three Japanese guards riding with them nudged each other and laughed.

The truck pulled up outside the small penal colony hospital at Iwahig, and Mac was carried inside to a makeshift surgical room—hardly a surgeon's delight—an empty room with one table placed in the center. By this time Mac's appendix had ruptured, and Doc Mango couldn't wait any longer. He asked the guards for anesthetics to put Mac under, but the "Nie Nie" answer from the smiling guards told him there were no anesthetics. "Anything! My God, don't you have any kind of ether to put this man to sleep?" he pleaded. Doc Mango paused, briefly assessing the situation, and then looked at Mac, "I'm gonna have to go ahead and cut ya like this, Mac. Hold tight, because it's gonna hurt like hell. If we don't get this thing out of ya immediately, you're gonna die, buddy!" Grimacing with pain, Mac snapped back at Mango, "We don't have any other choice do we, Doc? For Christ's sake go ahead and get on with it! It can't be much more pain than what I'm going through right now!"

The three guards from the barracks and two other guards from Iwahig swarmed around the table. Two guards held Mac's legs down, two held his arms, and the fifth held Mac's shoulders as Doc Mango moved into position, scalpel in hand. Mac felt Mango's first incision. It really didn't hurt as bad as he thought it would. Then it happened. It felt as if Mango were holding a hot poker to his stomach, and he let out a long scream of "Ohhhhhhh my God!" The guards holding Mac started laughing and making fun of his screams. Mac screamed, "Laugh, you stupid bastards!" From that point on, he dropped in and out of consciousness. Whenever he came out of it, he looked up to see the guards laughing at him. One of the guards grabbed his side yelling, "Oh, it hurt!" and then they all laughed.

The operation took about three hours. Doc Mango had done the best he could under the circumstances, and he began closing the incision, sewing it shut with some catgut he kept in his little black bag. Doctor, patient and guards stayed at Iwahig for two days, and then they loaded Mac into the back of the truck and headed back to Puerto Princesa.

It was late evening when the truck pulled into Palawan Barracks, and Smitty and Roy came running toward the truck. Smitty had a mile-wide grin on his face, and said, "Dole, you tough ol' rascal, I knew you'd make it!" Roy patted Mac on the shoulder and said, "Sure as hell nice to see ya back, Mac!" Mac was glad to be back, too, but he wasn't out of the woods just yet.

All of them helped carry him into the barracks, where he was placed on his blanket. Doc Mango looked at his incision one more time to make sure everything was okay, and what he saw, he didn't like. Infection had set in. Mango removed the sutures, poured hot water into the incision, cleaned out the infected area as best he could, and closed the incision again.

When it came to Mac's well-being, Smitty was a worrywart. He didn't think Mac was getting enough to eat. His rice ration had been cut because he wasn't working at the airfield, so Smitty sneaked in extra bits of food he'd acquired during the day, and he was constantly looking for more. Shortly after Mac had returned to the camp, Smitty and another POW were standing outside the barracks talking when Smitty spotted two chickens roosting on a fence post near the barbed wire. He told the other POW to grab one or both of them. The POW walked slowly toward the birds. He didn't want to excite them. Both were hens who helped provide Filipinos in the area with the roosters used in cock fighting, a national pastime in the Philippines. He slowly, very slowly slipped his arm through the barbed wire and held his hand out towards the two birds. Hard to believe what happened next. One of the birds jumped on his hand. He slowly pulled his arm through the wire and walked ever so slowly over to Smitty, who quickly snatched the chicken from his hand and ripped off its head. Running to the boiling tea barrel, he cooked it. A short time later, Smitty, the other POW and Mac were eating chicken. "Oh," Mac remembered later, "the meat tasted so good." It would be some time before he would be able to get up from his bed.

Two days after the chicken dinner, the infection returned. Doc Mango removed the sutures for the third time. Mac's flesh around the incision was so rotten that the catgut wouldn't hold his skin together. The smell of the rotting skin and fluids seeping from the incision was overwhelming. After removing the catgut, Mango took a good look into Mac's open incision and said, "Before I can sew you up again, Mac, we're gonna have to make sure this infection is out for good. If we have to remove the sutures again we'll never get anything to hold you together."

For three days Mac laid flat on his back with his insides hanging out on his blanket next to Smitty and Roy. Although his insides were exposed to flies, mosquitoes, dirt and other infectious invaders, it was the only way to clean the exposed organs. Three times a day Doc Mango would bring in a bowl of hot water and pour it into Mac's insides. Then, he'd stick his hand into the opening and wash the infection. Both Roy and Smitty helped. When they returned in the evening from their day at the airfield, Smitty would get more hot water, and he and Roy would perform the same task Mango had done throughout the day.

Mac could lie in only one position, on his back. By the third day with little or no movement, with bed sores starting to form on his tailbone, he could hardly stand the pain. Added to the pain of the open infection and the bedsores, he was thirsty, so thirsty he'd about given up. Smitty and Roy were fast asleep when Mac nudged Smitty who mumbled, "Whatcha need, Dole?" Mac looked up at Smitty, his voice clearly indicating his pain and frustration. "Listen my friend, I'm dying. You know it, and I know it. The whole goddamn place knows it. I'm so damned uncomfortable. Go get me some water! I'm so thirsty." Smitty was just as frustrated: "You can't have anything to drink with your insides hangin' out like that Dole. You know that!" "If you don't go get it," said Mac, "I'll crawl out of this damn place and get it myself!" Smitty gave in. Reluctantly he sneaked out of the barracks and returned with a canteen full of cold water. Mac grabbed it and drank the whole thing. Then he turned on his side to take some of the pressure off the sores on his back. "God, this feels good! Thanks, my friend." With that, he closed his eyes and went to sleep.

He woke up later that night when he felt something pop inside him. He placed his hand on his side and felt something seeping out of the incision. It was pus, and a lot of it. The smell was sickening. He was scared. He didn't know whether he'd live or die, but he felt a lot better. The infection was pouring out of his body, and he closed his eyes and went to sleep. For the first time since his appendix had burst, Mac fell into a deep sleep.

"What the hell do you think you're doing, Mac?" Doc Mango was angry. He'd walked into the barracks to check on Mac and, finding him on his side in a pool of slime, started yelling at him. Mac told him what he'd done and why he'd done it. Mango listened to him and then ran from the barracks, returning with another bowl of hot water. He started the cleaning process again. By this time, Mac was so sick of feeling Mango, Smitty and Roy's hands probing his open incision that he was about ready to give up, but Mango had good news: "All the infection is gone, Mac! It must have drained out." With a smile spreading across his face, Mango gave him the good news. "By God, McDole, I think you're gonna make it!"

For the next week, the washing routine continued. Smitty and Doc Mango rinsed his incision three times a day until Mango decided it was time to close the incision for the last time. By this time, the Doc had run out of catgut, and he begged the guards for more. All he got from them was, "Nie, nie." There had to be a way, and the good doctor found it. Looking at the buttons on Mac's shirt, a shirt he'd saved but never worn, Mango asked the guards for some string. They came up with string and more buttons. Mango took the buttons and began sewing them onto Mac's body, six on each side of the incision. He then pulled more string through the buttons and pulled them all together closing the incision. Mac was literally buttoned up.

The guards were amazed at what had happened, and they entered the barracks, two at a time, to look at his incision. When they'd ask him to let them see his buttoned-up body, he'd respond, "Nie, nie." They'd get mad and shove their bayonets in his face, telling him they would kill him if he didn't show them the incision. Mac yelled one word right back at them: "Tobacco!" The deal was made. Mac would get three or four cigarettes, and the guards would get a look at his buttoned-up body. If he didn't give the cigarettes to Smitty, he'd sell or trade them to other POWs for food. This helped supplement his ration of rice, which had been halved because he couldn't work.

Mac didn't smoke. He had no use for cigarettes, and he remembered his days on Corregidor, when he'd watch men in their foxholes rip pages from their bibles to roll homemade cigarettes. He couldn't understand how a man could trade precious food for a couple of cigarettes. When he received his cigarette ration, he'd put one behind each ear and walk by Smitty, who was a serious smoker. Then the chase would begin. "Dole, you ornery rascal, give me them smokes, or I'm gonna kill ya!" The chase would last for a minute or two, Mac would laugh as his nicotine-crazed buddy ran after him. Sometimes he'd give Smitty a couple of smokes, but most of the time he traded his cigarettes for food, figuring the cigarettes were probably saving his life because he had more food than the other prisoners.

When he was strong enough to walk around, he was given a job inside the Commandant's office. It only took him about 15 minutes a day to do the work, which required him to keep tabs on the prisoners who were working that day and those who were on sick call. With the prisoner roster in front of him, he decided to memorize the names and hometown of every prisoner in Palawan Barracks. It was a mental exercise for him—it kept his mind active—and at night in the barracks he'd go over and over the names, putting them in alphabetical order. This would be valuable information later in the war.

With little work to do and his buddies slaving away on the airfield, Mac couldn't help thinking about home. He thought a lot about his mother, Dessa. It was she who had signed the paper which had allowed him to join the Marines. He thought about the day he had come home from the recruiting office. He'd signed up, but he needed a parental signature. Even though he was nineteen, going on twenty, a parental signature was required in 1940, and he had decided to ask his mother to sign the consent form. It was lunchtime when he entered the house. His mother was in the kitchen. He handed her the paper and told her what he was going to do. He said it was something he had to do, that nothing would change his mind. Dessa McDole didn't say anything. She just kept looking at her son. Her chin began to quiver, and she was near tears. She reached for the paper and pen and signed her name. She didn't say a word. Mac's sisters began to cry. His oldest brother, Max, didn't know what to think, but figured Mac knew what he was doing. And as for his little brother, Joe, he was too young to understand. Mac returned the enlistment paper on Monday, raised his right hand and took the oath. It was November 4, 1940. He was now a United States Marine. When his dad and uncle Hayes returned from working out of state that evening, little Joe blurted out the news as the two men walked through the door. Glenn's father was sad when he heard what Glenn was going to do and didn't say much. He told Glenn he was sorry he wouldn't be able to see him off at the train station the next day, because he had another job lined up out of state. The elder McDole was near tears. He was losing his son, his favorite hunting buddy.

As he neared the end of his convalescence, there was another increase in the number of prisoners beaten while working at the airfield site. The POWs were being pushed to the limit. Smitty and Roy returned to the barracks at night drained of energy. One evening, Mac watched the prisoners return from the airfield, and several among them, including Smitty, were bruised and bloodied. "What in hell happened, Smitty? "Mac asked, as he helped Smitty to his mat. Smitty looked up at him and said, "I tell ya, Dole, Smiley just saved our lives." Mac gave Smitty a confused look and said, "Saved your lives? What in hell are ya talking about? What happened out there today?"

Wiping blood and sweat from his face, Smitty gave his account of what happened: "We were working in the field when they brought us out our chow. We had seen a bunch of bananas out in the jungle this morning, so we decided to go out and pick some when our lunch arrived. As soon as they yelled at us that chow was there, everyone dropped what they were doing and ran into the jungle to get the bananas. I don't know if the guards thought we were trying a mass escape or not, but they were madder than hell. I think they would have killed us for sure, but Smiley was one of the guards today, and he talked the other guards into the type of punishment he thought we should get. They made all seventy of us stand in two columns and take logs, boards, sticks, whatever they could find for us, and beat each other until we dropped."

It was now Mac's turn to help Smitty. He wiped away some of the blood with water from his canteen and then tended to the other wounds.

"Jesus, Smitty, you're a mess. Couldn't you take it easy on each other?" "Are you kidding, Dole? We couldn't even fake it. I'm sure if they thought we weren't hitting each other as hard as they thought we should be, they would have started in on us, or, worse yet, they would have shot or bayoneted us!" Mac tried joking. "Honest to Pete, Smitty, see the trouble you get in when I'm not around to help you?" Smitty, was in no mood for joking: "Sure, Dole, and since you're so damn good to me, go get me my chow and let me rest like you have all day!" Mac turned, walking toward the barracks door, and said, "Sure enough my friend, anything you say!" He turned at the barracks door and, grinning, added, "I bet you guys looked pretty foolish out there beating hell out of each other! Too bad I missed it." Smitty threw a blood-soaked rag at Mac as he stepped out the door.

Rooster

They called him "Rooster." Mac and the other prisoners didn't know his full name, his service affiliation, or his rank. It appeared the rigors and terror of war had had a devastating effect on him. He was in another world. The guards thought he was crazy and left him alone. He'd stand on the trunk of a tree that had just been felled by a POWs ax. He'd strut up and down the tree trunk, flapping his arms, and crow like a chicken. The guards thought he was funny and would give him a cigarette or two after one of his struts. Mac and the others couldn't help laughing, watching the crazy guy go through his routine. When the prisoners dallied too long during Rooster's performance, guards would crack a few heads to get them back to work. Rooster never let up. At night he could be heard crowing and cackling like a chicken at the other end of the barracks. No one knew whether he was crazy or whether it was an act, and they would never know. Rooster was shipped out of Palawan to Manila. No one knew what happened to him, but maybe he wasn't so crazy after all.

Late April, 1943

As Palawan's prisoners labored away, U.S. fighter-bombers were busy. Although the prisoners knew nothing of the events taking place in the Pacific, their guards, officers and other soldiers of the Japanese battalion did. The POWs didn't know that Japanese Admiral Yamamoto had been killed in late April of '43, when his plane was shot down by eighteen American fighter-bombers near Bougainville in the Solomon Islands. Or that at about the same time, the Japanese announced they had executed several captured American airmen held in Japan following the Doolittle Raid on Tokyo. The tension and animosity between guards and prisoners increased.

There were no more days off. Mac, Smitty and the POWs were working from dawn to dusk, seven days a week. By late April the future airfield had been cleared of trees and brush and had been leveled—it was as flat as a pool table. The sickly, exhausted prisoners of Palawan Barracks had cleared an area 210 meters by 2200 meters, over a mile and a half long. But there was more heavy work ahead. Two motorized cement mixers were pulled to the work site. One of them produced a yard of cement at a time, and the other a half-yard, hardly enough to construct a runway, but the two small machines would be augmented by prisoners mixing cement by hand in their wooden wheelbarrows. At any one time there were at least six crews mixing cement in wheelbarrows. In all, they were about to lay cement for a runway eight inches thick that would measure 1,400 meters long, with concrete turntables at each end. But that wasn't all. Turnoffs would be required to get the fighters and bombers to their revetments hidden in the jungle. In all, a truly massive undertaking for the prisoners of Palawan.

There were still some high spots in the coral base of the runway, which had to be flattened. Mac was pounding the coral with a sledgehammer one day when he accidentally hit Evan Bunn's hand. It was an ugly injury. Bunn's hand was bleeding, and the guard ran over to see what had happened. With all the blood pouring out of his hand, it looked to the guard as if Bunn had lost a thumb. It made the guard so angry that he whacked Mac over the head, believing he'd intentionally smashed Bunn's hand. Although bloodied and in pain, Bunn burst into laughter, telling the guard that his thumb had always been missing. The guard didn't take kindly to having been made a fool of, so he refused to let Bunn return to camp for first aid. Bunn worked the rest of the day with a broken and bleeding hand.

Cement is caustic, and in normal times, handling it requires the right clothing and footwear, to guard against it coming in contact with bare skin. The well-dressed POW of Palawan Barracks, wearing either shorts or a glorified jock strap, no shirt and homemade sandals, soon fell victim to the effects of working with and wading in cement. Huge ulcers began to eat away at their legs and feet. Complaints fell on deaf ears, so Mac fell back on his tried-and-true treatment, which consisted of soaking his legs in saltwater whenever he had the chance. Still, he wasn't as concerned about the leg and foot ulcers as about the cement dust they inhaled. He'd been forced to load and then unload the bulk cement from the hold of the ship when he arrived on Palawan, and now he was faced with daily exposure to the same dust for weeks on end. All he had to protect his lungs was a homemade bandanna, which covered his face. There was choking and coughing constantly while mixing the cement in their wheelbarrows or shoveling it into the two small motorized mixers.

As they labored away through the month of May, the Japanese ended their occupation of the Aleutian Islands after U.S. forces captured Attu.

June, 1943

The U.S. began all-out submarine warfare against the Japanese in the Pacific. On Palawan, the daily grind of hard labor and beatings continued. The Japanese were aware of what was happening to their transport ships as a result of increased American submarine patrols, and it was reflected in their treatment of the POWs. Work was from dawn to dusk, food wasn't any better, and the number of sick prisoners increased. There was a constant rotation of sick, useless prisoners out of Palawan and healthier ones imported from Manila to replace them.

Malarial attacks were increasing. The prisoner's diet and the long, hard work on the field slowly drained them of the ability to fight off diseases. Mac would have a malarial flare-up, and it would take about two or three days before the fever left; and then Smitty would be flat on his back for a couple of days. There was little, if anything, Doc Mango could do to keep them healthy. It was a vicious cycle. Once they recovered from a malarial bout, they knew they'd come down with it again in a couple of weeks.

Roy Henderson had a tougher time fighting off the attacks, and he became progressively weaker. In one of his last attacks, he'd been down for several days when they finally talked him into getting up and going through the chow line. He would have been better off staying on his sleeping mat. No sooner had the three stepped into line for their ration of rice than Roy got into a fight with another prisoner. The prisoner, known as "Hoot" Gibson, was a better fighter, and Roy ended up with a severe head injury. Mac and Smitty carried him to Doc Mango's sickbay. Mango took one look at Roy and knew he would never be able to work at the airfield again. Mango put Roy on the list of sick prisoners to be shipped to Manila.

Until the ship arrived, Mac and Smitty did all they could for Roy by sneaking fruits into the barracks, providing him with bananas or breadfruit. Roy was making a slow recovery, a very slow recovery. They worked his arms back and forth, exercising them as much as possible, then worked his legs, fearing that if they didn't exercise them, he'd never walk again.

Coconuts! That's what Roy needed, and they knew where they could get some, but there was risk involved. The coconuts were right in the

Five middle-aged survivors of the Palawan reunite long after the Pacific War had ended. From left: Glenn McDole, Roy Henderson, Rufus Smith, Clarence Clough and Evan Bunn.

middle of the prison courtyard—one big tree with dozens of ripe coconuts just waiting to be picked—and the man who volunteered for the job of shimmying up the tree and knocking the coconuts to the ground was Rufus Smith. Smitty could shinny up a coconut tree faster than any man in the camp. They waited until dark. Mac acted as lookout. If they were caught, both knew they'd be beaten and thrown in the dungeon. The big coconut tree was the only one in the compound which still had fruit on it. Mac counted 32 coconuts, and it would be Smitty's job to get them down. When it was all clear, Mac gave Smitty the signal, and he shimmied up the tree. Mac marveled at how fast Smitty could get to the top. He figured ol' Smitty was faster than any of the natives on the island. The operation was going smoothly, with about half the coconuts dropped to the ground and carried into the barracks, when there was a change of guards. It was bad timing. Mac gave Smitty a signal to stay where he was and wait it out. Changing of the guard takes time, and in this case it was a painful wait for Smitty. He had disturbed a hornets nest, and was stung numerous times all over his body as he waited for the guards to leave. He took the stings in silence, knowing that if he even whimpered, he'd likely be beaten to death.

When the guards left, Mac gave Smitty the all-clear. He kicked down the rest of the coconuts and shimmied down the tree. By this time, they had so many that they didn't have any place to hide them, so Evan Bunn and Clarence Clough came to their rescue by hiding the coconuts in their homemade locker. Roy Henderson had all the extra nourishment he needed to recover, but recovery was not something Mac and Smitty would see. To the Japanese, Roy Henderson was useless. He'd never be able to work on the airfield again. Doc Mango agreed, and Roy was sent back to Manila's Bilibid Prison. It was a big loss and a very sad occasion for him and his buddies. Working together, the three had survived some terrible times, and they knew there would be more to come. Smitty, especially, was affected by Henderson's departure. They had been together a long time, from the very beginning. Both were born and raised in small towns in east Texas (Hughes Springs and Hooks), and they had gone through boot camp together.

7

A Change of Command

There were some changes made at Palawan Barracks in June of '43. Captain Kishamoto, the camp's first commandant, was assigned to other duties in Manila. Mac believed Kishamoto had taken a liking to his prisoners because they never cracked up under pressure. Mac knew Kishamoto was the man who ordered the punishments, but, aside from that, the commandant and his prisoners got along pretty well. As for the beatings, the Iowa Marine considered them a fact of life at Puerto Princesa. Before he left Palawan, Kishamoto told them, "You be good soldiers and you will go home!"

Kishamoto was replaced by Captain Kinoshita, a little man about five and a half feet tall, who probably weighed no more than 120 pounds. Mac figured he must have been about sixty years old, at least he looked it. No one saw much of Kinoshita after he arrived. He didn't make speeches and didn't appear when the men were called to formation in front of the barracks. But the guards he brought with him made their presence known. They were tough and mean. All carried hardwood batons about a yard long, and they didn't hesitate to use them. Beatings increased when Kinoshita took command, and the prisoners suspected there would be rough times ahead of them.

Although there were a lot of new guards, the POWs still had Smiley. Mac and Smitty didn't see him as often, because he was assigned to other guard duties. Mac's crew lucked out when a guard they called "Blinky" was assigned to them. Blinky didn't look for trouble, wasn't a harsh overseer, and he appeared to be as dumb as a rock. Occasionally, they'd get another guard, who they called "John the Baptist" to his face. They would tell him what a wonderful man he was, and the guard would give them a pleasant smile and nod in appreciation. But, out of hearing range, they called him "John the Bastard." He wasn't a nice guy, and never spared the club.

Although Mac and the other prisoners knew nothing about what was happening outside Palawan Island, they did have a feeling that the war was going their way. Their first indication was the presence of the front-line troops who came to the island with Kinoshita. About a week after Kinoshita arrived, the prisoners were heading out for another day of cement work at the airfield when a Filipino native riding a bicycle passed them on the road. He pedaled slowly, and in a hushed voice he kept repeating, "Won't be long now, Joe. Won't be long now!" Those that heard those words were jubilant ... but subdued. They didn't want to stir up the guards. There was a lot of whispering and a few smiles as they marched to work. Mac glanced toward Smitty and in a hushed voice said, "By God, we're right, Smitty! This stinking war is almost over." Smitty's first thought, and Mac's, too, was of food. "My lips are already watering for some fried chicken, Dole. How 'bout you?" A big steak and a bottle of beer didn't enter his mind at that time, but that night in the barracks he dreamed of an angel food cake topped with a big glob of ice cream.

June 16, 1943, was a day to remember at the McDole home in Urbandale. A War Department telegram was delivered to Mac's parents informing them their son was alive and a prisoner of war in the Philippines. The family was told they could write to him in care of the Japanese Red Cross in Tokyo, via the American Red Cross in New York City. There was a celebration in the McDole household that day.

There was yet one more attempt at a break for freedom in the prison camp. It occurred June 28, 1943, when a Marine private, Seldon White, and a Navy prisoner, Earl Vance Wilson, sneaked into the jungle. When their escape was discovered, all the prisoners working at the airfield were marched back to the barracks and made to stand at attention for three hours. They were dismissed when the Japanese decided that none of the prisoners knew about or had helped in the prisoners' escape.

White and Wilson managed to evade capture for six days, but on July 4, they were captured and returned to Palawan Barracks. A pitiful sight awaited the POWs when they returned from work at the airfield that day. White and Wilson were squatting just outside the guardhouse. Their hands were tied behind their backs, and it was evident they had been beaten. Their heads were bloodied and their bodies bruised. Then, the man who enjoyed torturing prisoners more than any guard at Palawan, Taichi Deguchi, put on a show for the POWs. Everyone was called to formation and forced to watch as Deguchi beat the stooped and bloodied prisoners about the head and body. It was the most brutal beating up to that time.

After the demonstration, the two escapees, unable to walk, were

Japanese allegedly responsible for the burning, shooting, bayoneting, and murdering of 139 American POW's on Palawan Island, P.I., during a fake air raid in 1944 are on trial before the Yokohama War Crimes Commission in Yokohama, Japan (U.S. War Department).

dragged to the brig, where they were held for three days without food or water. On the fourth day, Deguchi and other soldiers in his unit loaded them on a truck and took them out of camp. They were never seen again. Filipinos later passed word to the prisoners that White and Wilson had been taken to the airfield, where they had been shot and buried. Their graves were never found by the prisoners who worked at the construction site.

The Japanese commander laid down the law after receiving orders from Manila about what to do when a man escaped. This time, all the POWs were lined up and made to count off, and it was clear the Japanese would carry out Manila's orders. Mac and the others formed into squads of ten men each, and they made a pact: no one would try to escape, or if all of them agreed, they would escape together. Replacements coming into Palawan Barracks from Manila knew of several executions carried out at other POW camps. In one instance, a prisoner reportedly watched as his brother was lined up with other prisoners and executed.

Shortly after the edict, Corporal Charles Street lost his way returning to the barracks from the airfield. While he was stumbling around in the bush, looking for a way back to the barracks, the Japanese figured another prisoner had escaped. They rounded up the nine men in Street's unit and threw them all in the brig, where they were beaten. They went a step further than usual and used iron pipes to beat the men. All the battered, bloodied prisoners believed they'd soon be standing in front of a firing squad. Meanwhile, Street found his bearings and headed back to camp. When he walked through the gate, the guards released the men in the brig and grabbed Street, throwing him into a cell where he was also beaten. There was no doubt among the prisoners that, had Street not returned, the nine men in his unit would have been shot.

The prisoners were edgy and nervous. The daily ration of rice had been cut, and with the arrival of the new prison commander, the guards delighted in showing the prisoners just how mean and tough they were. There was still talk of escape. Mac overheard three POWs talking about an escape plan. "Foolproof!" he heard them say. His temper showed itself again. Mac walked over to them and said, "I'll kill the three of you right here with my bare hands before I'll let thirty men die because of you!" They saw Mac's anger, and one of them said, "Okay, Mac, just settle down." There was no more talk of escape.

Although escape at this point seemed impossible, there was a way for some to evade work at the airfield. For the prisoner who failed, there was a bloody price to be paid. One of the prisoners was known as the "Arm Breaker." Mac didn't like him, called him a "sadistic bastard." He loved to inflict pain and was always looking for a fight. Shortly after he arrived on Palawan, he had picked the wrong man to fight with, had gotten into it with the camp's strongman, Jack Taylor. Taylor was the man who had received a horrendous beating from Japanese guards during the corned beef incident, "He beat the shit out of the Arm Breaker," Mac said later of Taylor.

The Arm Breaker was paid in either cigarettes or extra food for breaking arms. It was a simple procedure. The prisoner laid his arm over a log, and the Arm Breaker used a heavy metal pole to break the bone. One big whack usually did it. The prisoners who succeeded in making their broken arms look like an accident were shipped back to Manila. Those who didn't get away with it received an additional beating, brig time and half the amount of rice it took to survive. Doc Mango set the broken arms as best he could using splints—no such luxury as a plaster cast—and the injured men went back to work on the airfield.

Little things, sometime innocent answers to simple questions, could trigger rage among the guards, especially Manichi Nishitoni. The camp cook, who oversaw food preparation for not only the prisoners, but also for Japanese officers and men, had a hair-trigger temper. Three POWs—

one of Mac's buddies, Doug Bogue, and prisoners Bingham and Schraub—
had been given the job of making and then hauling tea to the men working on the airfield. Nishitoni was supervising. He asked Bingham what he
thought of Japanese food. The POW told Nishitoni that the fish and rice
diet wasn't too popular back home. "Americans," he said, "like meat and
potatoes." An innocent reply, but Nishitoni exploded. He grabbed a five-
gallon can of boiling water and threw it on the prisoner's leg. There wasn't
much Bogue and Schraub could do for Bingham. When they removed his
shoe, the skin came off his foot. Doc Mango did what he could, applying
what bandages he had to the burned foot and lower leg. In a few days the
leg started to swell and became infected. For a while, Mango thought he'd
have to amputate. He made one more attempt to save the leg, and it
worked. He removed as much of the dead skin as he could from the man's
foot and leg, popping blisters as big as a man's hand, and drained out as
much of the infection as he could. Prisoner Bingham was back at work
hauling hot tea to the airfield about a week after he was scalded. He walked
gingerly on that foot.

Private First Class George Waddell was from Kansas City. He was
well-liked among the other POWs and could best be described as a cool
sort of guy. Waddell had a stiff middle finger on his left hand. It would not
bend. Anytime a guard came around he'd light up a cigarette and place it
in his left hand so it looked as if he was "giving the finger" to the guard.
New guards at the airfield took offense at what they saw and threatened a
beating if he didn't bring the finger down. Waddell had a look of inno-
cence, and he was very apologetic, very submissive toward the guards,
explaining that his middle finger had been broken and it would not bend.
That seemed to satisfy them. When they walked off, Waddell switched the
cigarette to his right hand. This always drew snickers and choked laughs
from Mac and the rest of the crew. All of them thought George Waddell
was a good man.

Mac and the rest of his crew got a break from inhaling cement dust
and walking in wet cement. Construction work at the airfield needed more
water, and Mac's crew of ten men was assigned to lay another water pipe
down the mountain. It wasn't easy, but it was better than working all day
in a cloud of cement dust. Blinky, a guard Mac and the others were comfortable with, was assigned to the work party. The prisoners knew he wasn't
the brightest guy in the world and never said much while watching over
them. His eyes blinked constantly. He was no threat.

They were trucked to the work site, and as they rode up the mountain, they talked about escape. It was always on their minds. Blinky paid
no attention as they talked, his face was always a blank. It was J. O. Warren who first said they could make a break for it and wouldn't get caught.

"We could kill Blinky, steal the truck and be gone before anyone knew it. With the truck, we'd be able to move real fast," he said. They all looked at each other and, suddenly, Smitty grabbed Blinky from behind and put one of his arms around the guard's neck. Blinky's expression changed the moment Smitty's arm tightened. They could tell he was frightened. He had the look of a man who knew he was about to die. He said nothing as he stared at the prisoners, his eyes blinking rapidly. Smitty's arm, locked tightly over Blinky's windpipe, caused him to breath in short gasps. Smitty looked at the others and said, "We've got a full tank of gas and the truck is runnin' good. Just let me know what you want to do." There was a brief pause, and then Smitty remembered that Evan Bunn and Clarence Clough were back at camp. He paled, muttered, "My God, they're three numbers below us." An escape meant Bunn and Clough would be shot. Smitty released his grip on Blinky's neck, spun him around and said, "You better watch it from now on, 'cause we can still get to you anytime we want!"

When the work had been finished on the mountainside and the prisoners returned to Palawan Barracks, nothing more was said. For months, the memory of that day stayed with them. As for Blinky, he was happy to be alive, and he never reported the incident to his superiors.

Late Summer, 1943

An increasing tide of American planes, ships, Army and Marine units continued to push across the Pacific. B-24 Liberators from Midway had bombed Wake Island; in the Solomon Islands, it was the battle of Vella Gulf; and U.S. forces overwhelmed the Japanese on New Georgia. The POWs of Palawan, oblivious to events beyond the island, continued work on an airfield that was just beginning to take shape.

Puerto Princesa's rainy season—if you could call it that—occurred during the late summer and early fall. But it didn't slow work on the airstrip. On the days when the prisoners couldn't pour cement, there were two dirt runways, which straddled the uncompleted cement runway, that had to be leveled. Rain never stopped work on those projects.

Richard Packer, one of Mac's buddies from boot camp, was shipped to Palawan as a replacement for one of the many POWs too sick or too weak to work. Mac had become buddies with Packer and a man named Roy Bean in boot camp in San Diego. They'd crossed the Pacific together on the USS Showmont, stopping briefly in Honolulu for their very first shore leave since they'd joined the Marines. They'd had a great time watching sailors and soldiers going in and out of Honolulu's whorehouses. They had retreated to the beach, where they spent time ogling young women and pitching coins into the water for young Hawaiian boys, who were expert at diving for the coins. After the beach foray and shore duty as MPs, they had boarded the Showmont for the remainder of the trip to the Philippines.

Shortly after Packer arrived at the prison camp, he came down with malaria. The prisoners did what they could for him. His temperature climbed so high that they couldn't get a reading on Doc Mango's thermometer and all Packer could do was lie on his mat and shake. He was shaking so violently that they covered him with blankets and then took turns lying on top of him to keep him warm. Nothing seemed to work.

Mac had an idea—a last resort, he thought, but it might work. He picked up Packer in his arms and carried him to a vat of rainwater not far from the barracks. It was about six feet across and five feet deep. Mac put Packer in the vat and held him in the water for about ten minutes. Mac figured it would either cure Packer or kill him. Doc Mango saw what Mac had done and ran to the vat screaming, "Are you crazy, Mac? Jesus, you're gonna kill him!" He told the Doc why he had done it, and both were surprised when Packer quit shaking and his temperature dropped to near normal. From then on, Doc Mango took all his fever-ridden patients to the water tank. It became common practice for all the prisoners whose temperatures topped the thermometer to take a dip in the water tank.

There were no disruptions in construction of the airfield during the late summer and fall of '43. The Japanese seemed satisfied with the overall progress. With modern equipment, the field could have been completed much earlier. American Seabees constructed airfields on liberated islands in the Pacific in less than a week, and in some cases laid steel matting for a landing strip in one day. But 300 men, many of them sick, using only simple tools—picks, shovels, wooden wheelbarrows, and two very small cement mixers—could do no more. The work continued, day in and day out, from sun-up to sunset. Once a month, the prisoners wasted by the hard work and disease were shipped back to Manila to be replaced by new, healthier laborers.

In September of '43, Navy Boatswain's Mate Jim Flynn became the first and only casualty during construction of the airfield. A Japanese Zero made an emergency landing on one of the dirt runways. Mac watched as it ran off the runway, its prop striking and killing Flynn. It wasn't much of a burial. Some of the prisoners made a wooden cross and, using a mess kit knife, carved his name on it. Father Reyes, a priest at the church in Puerto Princesa, conducted the burial service. There were a few words and a prayer, and then burial in the town cemetery.

There was always someone thinking of escape. Even with the threat of a firing squad for the escapees and the others in their work unit, Walt Ditto of Des Moines and Robert May managed to communicate with a Filipino while working at the airfield. Their escape plan was simple enough: they would go under the barbed wire and move down the huge embankment to the bay. There, the Filipino would be waiting in his small canoe to take them to the southern tip of the island and freedom in what was called the "Free Philippines." It would have been a 100-mile canoe trip down the coast.

Somehow Manichi Deguchi got wind of the plot. He found one of the notes Ditto and May sent to the Filipino. Both prisoners were dragged out of the morning lineup and whisked off to the camp's brig. Deguchi had both men strung up by their wrists. The beatings they endured were ferocious, and they were beaten nearly every day of their three-month sentence in the camp's dungeon. Denied adequate food and water, the two prisoners were near death when they were dragged out of the brig, placed on board a ship and sent back to Manila and Bilibid Prison. From Bilibid, they were put aboard a transport ship sailing to Japan and spent the rest of the war as slave laborers in Japanese coal mines.

Marine Private First Class Donald Thomas, a quiet, friendly farm boy from Macksburg, Iowa, had decided to see the world after he graduated from high school in 1939. Young Thomas drove into Des Moines, walked into the Navy/Marine enlistment office, and signed up. Because of his age, he needed parental approval, so he drove back to the farm and told his father he'd just joined the Navy and needed his permission. Donald's dad looked at the papers and said, "Son, you didn't join the Navy. You joined the United States Marine Corps." When Donald had walked into the enlistment office, he had seen a sign which read, "USMC," but he didn't understand what the letters meant. It didn't seem to bother Don Thomas, and a few months later he was a U.S. Marine Corps Seagoing Marine, stationed aboard the Cruiser, *U.S.S. Houston*. Thomas was one of the first Seagoing Marines to be under six feet tall. That had been a requirement for Seagoing Marines, but the Corps was running out of tall men. The *Houston* was in Manila Harbor when the Japanese bombed Pearl Harbor. When it headed out to sea to avoid certain destruction by Japanese bombs, the Marines on board, including Thomas, were transferred to land duty with the 4th Marine Regiment.

Thomas was a rifleman on Corregidor and had been there when Japanese troops stormed ashore on Bottomside. During the fighting, he had received a shrapnel wound to the leg and was taken to Corregidor's hospital in the huge Malinta Tunnel, where they patched him up and gave him a shot which put him to sleep. When he awoke and was able to walk out of the tunnel, he was a prisoner of war. For some unexplainable reason, the two Japanese soldiers who stood guard over him in the tunnel had offered him a cigarette, which he took.

Thomas, along with Mac, Smitty, Henderson, and thousands of other prisoners, had made the long walk up Dewey Boulevard to Bilibid Prison. He took the same death train to Cabanatuan as the other prisoners and later ended up on a small transport ship heading for Palawan's Prison Camp #10A, or Palawan Barracks.

Like Mac, Thomas was self-reliant and quickly learned how to survive the brutality of Palawan Barracks. He worked hard at the airstrip, figuring it was only a matter of time before American war planes would be using it as a landing field. He was right. Like all the other prisoners, he was knocked around from time to time. He received his share of the clubbing but was fortunate to be working for an older guard and a Japanese engineer who was in charge of airstrip construction. The engineer, a civilian and not imbued with the Bushido, or warrior code, looked the other way when Thomas would sneak off into the jungle to gather bananas. What he didn't eat right away, the engineer stored in his tool kit for future consumption. Not only was Thomas self-reliant and enterprising, he was very lucky.

Once the land was cleared and the leveling and paving of the airstrip had begun, Thomas built the wood forms used for laying the cement. When the workday ended for him at the airstrip, he spent his time sewing new soles on the prison guards' boots. That's why the other prisoners called him "The Cobbler." He wasn't given the material needed to repair what few boots were still in use among the prisoners of Palawan. By this time, most of the prisoners wore rubber-tire sandals or wooden slats. When necessary, he'd help repair the sandals or make new ones—that is, if an old rubber tire was available.

After nearly a year and a half in captivity, the prisoners were beginning to understand a little bit of the Japanese language. Some, including Mac, were able to have limited conversations with the guards. And if, by chance, they didn't understand a command, a clubbing by the guard usually got the desired results.

Christmas, 1943

Christmas Day of 1943 would never be forgotten by Mac. It was the day he received a Red Cross package from home. His mother, Dessa, had sent him a package containing Colgate toothpaste and what Mac later called, "some pretty, white T-shirts." Not having had anything so clean and new in nearly two years, he couldn't bring himself to wear them. He knew the shirts would be ruined in no time if he wore them to work, so he would take them out at night, before the lights went out, and look at them—something nice and clean—a reminder of home.

The Red Cross also included drugs and medicines in the package, but the prisoners never saw them. The Japanese removed the drugs, leaving only some gauze and adhesive tape. All in all, it was better than nothing.

The contents of Smitty's Christmas package set off howls of laughter in the barracks. When he opened the package and looked inside, he burst into laughter. Mac asked, "What in hell is so funny, man?" Smitty could hardly control himself. "Can you believe this?" he yelled, as he pulled the items—a shiny blue pair of swimming trunks and white bed sheets—out of the package. "Where in hell do they think we're at, a Boy Scout camp for the week?" He was laughing so hard tears were running down his cheeks, and then everybody joined in. "Christ! We don't even have beds to put these sheets on!" he bellowed. By this time, Smitty and Mac were all but rolling on the floor laughing. Mac suggested Smitty talk the guards into building a swimming pool, so he could use his swim trunks.

When the laughing died down, Smitty got serious. "Ya know, if I ever knew of anyone stuck in a hellhole like this, the only thing I'd send him would be food or cigarettes. Having smokes means the difference between life and death, and they're worth more than a hundred dollars." They all sat quietly for a moment nodding in agreement. Smitty was right. Mac, a non-smoker, had thought about it before. If his mom and dad had sent him some smokes, he would be rich. "Can you imagine," he thought, "what those Nips would give for some American cigarettes?"

Camp barber J. O. Warren was the next one to examine his package, which already had been opened by the guards. As he pulled out the contents, the expression on the faces of the guards changed, and they stepped back from their positions and put their rifles at port arms. There were two boxes of what appeared to be shotgun shells in the package. Warren pulled the boxes out of the package, knowing full well that other guards had opened them, so there was no need to fear what was inside. He couldn't believe what was stuffed in the shotgun boxes: the folks back home had made it a great day for him. The boxes were stuffed with chewing tobacco, something Warren loved and had hungered for during the long months of his imprisonment. He grabbed a chunk of the tobacco, bit into it and started chewing. The guards moved in closer. They had never seen chewing tobacco, and they asked for some of it. Warren obliged them. He gave them each a piece of the tobacco. He told them to put it into their mouths and chew and, then, when their mouths were full of juice, to swallow it. "Tastes better than saki," Warren boasted.

The guards followed Warren's instructions to the letter, and the reaction was immediate. As they swallowed the tobacco juice, there was a look of shock and revulsion as the juice surged down their throats. They began choking, spitting out what they could, choking some more and then vomiting. Just what J. O. Warren wanted. Sickness led to rage, and Warren's pleading reply was, "You have to acquire a taste for it. I just don't understand why you got sick." To avoid a beating he chewed a big hunk of the tobacco, and acted as if he had swallowed the juice. It worked. The guards, pale of face and sick to their stomachs, walked away.

Smitty's Christmas sheets weren't wasted. Mac took the sheets and ripped them apart. He took some old cable wire apart and used a strand as a needle. In no time at all, Mac had turned out four pairs of shorts, two for Smitty and two for him. And as for the swimming trunks, Smitty never wore them. It was something from home, and he was content to wear the shorts Mac had fashioned.

Shortly after Christmas, a letter from home sent Corporal Glenn McDole's morale sky-high. If was the first and only letter he'd received through the Red Cross since the war started. His kid sister, Dolores, sent him the following:

> Hi Glenn. We miss you so much and pray for your return soon. The pancakes are still waiting on the griddle for you. Tonight I'm going out with Johnny Sirfus. I know you don't know him, but he works at Boyt Harness with mom. His mom's name is Mrs. Mary Sirfus. I love you and hope to see you soon. Love, Dolores

He couldn't have been happier, the happiest he'd been in over two years, and he let the camp know it. He ran all over the compound talking and showing the letter and telling everyone who would listen to what it said. There were no strangers, he wanted the whole camp to know what he'd received. Mac ran up to Pop Sirfus, an Army musician who had been nearing retirement when he was captured by the Japanese on Corregidor. "Isn't that something, Pop?" Mac said. "I never knew we had any Sirfuses in Des Moines." Pop Sirfus looked at Mac, then sat down and started crying. "What the hell you cryin' for, Pop?" Mac asked. Pop Sirfus then told him this story: He and his wife, Mary, had separated a long time ago, and over the years they had drifted apart. He'd heard his former wife had moved to Iowa, but they hadn't corresponded. It was his son, Johnny, said Pop, who was dating Mac's sister.

The day after Mac's letter from home, a guard forced a prisoner to climb a coconut tree to knock down a ripe coconut. The prisoner was holding onto one of the tree's branches when it broke, and he plunged to the ground, snapping his spine. He lived for a few days and died on New Year's Day, '44. Father Reyes conducted his second funeral service for the POWs, burying the prisoner in the town's cemetery.

By the time Mac and his buddies had celebrated their Chrismas on Palawan, there had been huge allied advances in the Pacific and in Europe.

A victim of the Palawan massacre, Charlie (Pop) Sirfus, of Des Moines. Sirfus was due for retirement shortly after the war broke out. His two sons, John and Richard, still live in Des Moines.

In late 1943, U.S. Marines had invaded Cape Gloucester, battles were underway in the Solomon Islands, and Emperor Hirohito had told his coun-
trymen that the situation was "truly grave." In Europe, Italy had
surrendered and declared war on Germany. On the Eastern Front, the Ger-
mans were learning, as Napoleon did, what a Russian winter was like.

There were no New Year's resolutions by the Japanese guards to be kinder
overseers. The beatings, part of the daily routine at the prison camp, continued. Two prisoners who had been put on light duty because of malaria
and beriberi were next to feel Nishitoni's wrath. Working behind the barracks in the galley, they saw a papaya lying between strands of the barbed
wire fence. They reached through the wire to take it, and Nishitoni saw them
and went into a rage. He took them into the barracks and began beating
them. Using a heavy metal pole, he pounded them on the arms, buttocks and
backs until he was so exhausted he couldn't lift his club. Each man had both
of their arms broken. Doc Mango did what he could for them.

The prisoners hadn't had a bath in a long time. When they had first
arrived on Palawan, the guards had taken them to the beach after work
and let them wash the grime off their bodies, but there hadn't been any
beach bathing for some time. About twenty prisoners, including Mac and
Smitty, were sitting in the barracks complaining about their physical condition. Dirt, grime, cement dust and salt from perspiration had encrusted
their bodies, and the number of skin sores had increased. All of them
decided it was bath time, and they almost got away with it. They slipped
out behind the barracks to the big rainwater tank. They jumped in, and
the water felt good as it soaked into the crust. They had begun washing it
off their bodies when Nishitoni heard them. He ran to the vat and ordered
them out of the tank at rifle point. They were marched single-file to the
camp brig, and as they passed Nishitoni, he clubbed each man in the back
All of them spent two days in the brig without food or water.

Nishitoni was a complex figure, and not to be explained. A cruel,
sadistic man who would kill or torture at the drop of a hat, he seemed to
enjoy his role and played it to the hilt. When guards captured a wild pig
in the jungle and brought it back to camp, Nishitoni pulled his saber from
its scabbard and began slashing the pig, starting first at the genitals. As the
prisoners watched, a sort of crazed look appeared on his face. He slashed
into the pig harder, and his laughter grew louder with every downward
swing of the blade. Mac looked at Smitty, both of them shocked by the
bloody show Nishitoni was putting on, and Mac whispered, "This Jap is
an absolute maniac." Nishitoni then took the bloody, cut up carcass and
held it in his arms, wiping the blood on his face. Every prisoner watching
stood there quietly, mouths open, staring at the maniac in front of them.
When it was over, Nishitoni took the pig and walked away.

The meager rice diet was taking its toll on the prisoners in more ways than one. J. O. Warren was going blind, and it became worse every day. The prisoners didn't know if their diet was the cause, but the fact remained that Warren was going blind. They tried to help him. One of the men found some clear fiberglass while foraging in the town and tried shaping it and polishing it with powder. They found some wire, punched some holes at the edge of the lenses and Warren had a pair of wire-rimmed glasses. The homemade glasses didn't help much, but Warren seemed satisfied.

The prisoners came in from the airfield at dusk after another long day of mixing and pouring cement, and they were tired and dirty. Mac and Smitty hadn't entered the barracks yet when a half-dozen prisoners who slept under mosquito netting on the far side of the barracks walked outside and quietly asked them to come inside. They had something to show them. Mac and Smitty's curiosity piqued as they entered the barracks. They walked back to the group's sleeping area. One of the prisoners who'd invited them in said, "We have something to show you, but you can't tell anyone else, or I know we'll all get killed." Mac and Smitty were on edge as they watched the prisoner reach into his sea bag, something he'd managed to keep through all the long months as a captive. Both of them wondered what could be so precious that possessing it could mean a death sentence.

He slowly, carefully, pulled the package out of the sea bag, and Mac was astonished at what he saw, saying, "My God, where in hell did you get her at?" There were tears in his eyes as he looked at Old Glory displayed right in front of him. He wasn't the only one shedding tears; fact is, almost every man standing there could have used a handkerchief. As he wiped his eyes clear, he remembered how odd the prisoner had acted whenever anyone got near his sea bag. Now, he knew why. It was a beautiful flag, and they stood there for a while looking at it and not saying a word. Finally, fearing they might get caught, the prisoner carefully placed the flag back in the bottom of his sea bag. "I sleep with her every night," he said and closed the bag as the men walked away. A few of them still had tears in their eyes.

8

Goodbye to Old Friends

The next several months slipped by without incident. The daily beatings continued, but the Japanese were careful not to take them too far. They couldn't get much work out of a man with a broken body. By August of '44, the airstrip was nearly complete. What was supposed to have been a three-month work project had turned into two years of hard labor for the 300 prisoners of Palawan, and there was still more work to be done.

What the prisoners had accomplished up to that point would have been an unbelievable undertaking in the western world. Working with only hand tools, wheelbarrows and two small cement mixers (one that turned out a yard of cement per loading, the other only half that), and one rolling machine, it was a huge undertaking. The 300 men had labored for two years through malaria, beriberi, pellagra, a host of jungle funguses and other ailments, and the constant threat of severe punishment or death by their Japanese guards. They had cleared an area 2,400 yards by 225 yards and paved a runway measuring 1,530 yards by 75 yards. They had paved cement turnarounds at each end of the runway and built turnoffs for taxiing to the revetments.

When the airfield was nearly complete, life changed for the Palawan prisoners. On September 8, 1944 there was a third and final change of command, and a reduction in the number of prisoners in the camp. Captain Kinoshita was transferred to another post, taking all the officers and men who had served under him, including Blinky, one of the prisoners' favorite guards. Kinoshita was replaced by Lieutenant Sato, a short, thin little man with beady eyes, who probably weighed no more than 120 pounds. The prisoners called him "The Buzzard," and he would live up to his nickname.

On September 22, 1944, half of the camp's prisoners, 150 men, were put aboard a ship and sent to Manila, where many of them would be transferred to other slave labor camps operated by the Japanese. Basically, the Japanese had divided the prisoners into two companies, A and B. For those whose names appeared on the A list, it meant a trip to Manila, where they would board prison ships heading toward Japan. For men of B Company, it meant doom. Those who remained waved goodbye to their buddies as they marched out the gate and to the ship waiting for them at Puerto Princesa's docks.

One of those leaving Palawan was the camp's cobbler, Donald Thomas. The Macksburg, Iowa, farm boy was shipped back to Manila with the others and was one of hundreds packed in the hold of a rusty, slow moving transport ship, the *Haro Maru*. It was a death ship. It zigzagged across the Pacific to Japan to evade U.S. submarines. The prisoners were denied adequate food, water or even space enough to sit down. It was pandemonium in the hold. Prisoners began screaming. Panic set in. Finally, they heard the voice of a Catholic priest who had managed to climb to one of the steel beams above the prisoners. He began singing *Silent Night*. This quieted the prisoners.

In the black, stinking hold, the weaker prisoners began dying, and as each dead man was hoisted topside to be thrown overboard, there was a little more room below deck. There was little food or drinking water, no sanitary facilities, and no light in the hold, which reeked with the smell of urine and feces. The most important item a man had in that black, stinky hold was his canteen cup. If he didn't have that, he'd die of thirst. When they lowered the water or weak tea into the hold, the canteen was the only tool they had which would hold liquids. Fights to the death broke out in the hold when a canteen was stolen. It took nearly two months for the slow-moving ship to reach Formosa. The prisoners remained there for another three months recuperating from the ordeal before boarding the transport to their final destination.

The death ship finally dropped anchor at Wakayama, a small port city in Japan. Cobbler Thomas slaved away in a Japanese steel mill until American submarines and ships had cut off all raw material to the island nation. Then he was taken into the countryside, where the farm boy was right at home. He wasn't baling hay or planting corn, but spent his time working in the rice fields.

Mac and Smitty were sorry to see all of their old comrades leave, especially their two bunkmates, Clarence Clough and Evan Bunn. When Clough and Bunn walked out the gate, they were put aboard ship and eventually ended up working in the coal mines in Japan. Those left behind on Palawan whom Mac and Smitty considered close friends were Doug

Bogue, Doc Mango, Doctor Knight, Pop Daniels, Pop Sirfus, Charles Street, Carl Walker, Doug Burnett, "Rubber" Seagraves, C.C. Waddell and J. O. (John) Warren.

As they sat in their now half-empty barracks, Mac, Smitty, Carl Walker and John Warren talked about the day the year before when they'd almost made a run for freedom while on a work detail in the jungle. They quietly discussed their near attempt. All believed they could have made it to freedom, even though their guard, Blinky, would have been killed.

A few days after the prisoners had left the island, guards ran through the camp telling the remaining prisoners how lucky they were. The ship carrying their buddies back to Manila, the guards said, had been torpedoed and all aboard were lost. Gloom enveloped the camp for several days until a Filipino scout got close enough to let them know that their friends had actually made it safely to Manila. Later, though, many of their buddies, bound for slave labor in Japanese coal mines, drowned when their transport ship was torpedoed by an American submarine. Richard Packer, Mac's boot camp buddy, was one of the victims.

Life did not change for the better when The Buzzard took command of Palawan Barracks. Rations were cut. Mess kits once full of rice were now cut in half, and the rice was buggy and wormy. But it had always been wormy and buggy. The prisoners had been through this before, and they adjusted to what was now one full mess kit of rice per day. In addition to the rice, The Buzzard also made sure they had a side dish of soup—Comote (Philippine sweet potato) vines boiled in sea water. The soup didn't help a bit, and they were losing more weight and getting weaker. They'd take every chance they could to gather fruit from the jungle, and a good coconut was a prize.

With Lieutenant Sato came another group of seasoned guards to watch over the prisoners. There was Shubakii, a small man who carried brass knuckles and used them frequently on the prisoners. When he lashed out, he always tried to hit them in the mouth. Then there was Kawakini, an ex-fighter who had little patience and used his boxing skills to beat prisoners senseless. Although Kawakini enjoyed his work, Deguchi and Nishitoni were still considered to be the meanest, rottenest sons of bitches in the prison camp.

Life at Palawan Barracks had always been brutal and, with the arrival of the front-line troops and new guards, it was even worse. McDole and the other prisoners had formerly been allowed to seek shade while they ate lunch at the airfield, but no more. Under the new rules, they were given fifteen minutes to eat while standing in the sun, and there were no rest periods. They labored from dawn to dusk, seven days a week.

In addition to the change of command, other Japanese troops were moving onto Palawan Island. The 1,800-man 131st battalion of the Japanese 2nd Air Division would be responsible for the defense and maintenance of the airfield, which was now the second largest in the Philippines. All the Japanese soldiers and airmen were billeted in abandoned homes in Puerto Princesa, and all were seasoned front-line troops who had performed throughout Japan's long war in the Pacific and Asia.

From mid- to late 1944, the prisoners knew that American and Allied military might was rolling across the Pacific like a tidal wave. The Japanese began digging new revetments for artillery pieces along the shoreline and installing antiaircraft guns around the docks and the airfield. As for the prisoners, there was still more work to be done on the field and revetments to be built for the hundreds of fighter aircraft which would be stationed there. In late October of '44, the U.S. 6th Army invaded Leyte in the Philippines, while at sea the U.S. Navy scored a big victory in the Battle of Leyte Gulf. The Palawan prisoners had no idea U.S. forces were that close.

He was a little man, a Filipino scout, with a huge scar from his left cheekbone to his chin. His name was Pedro Pajie (pronounced "pay-hoe"). He came to the camp with gifts for the Japanese—rice cookies and saki— and he showed up almost every day. Mac hated him, as did all the other prisoners. Pajie laughed at and spit on the prisoners every chance he got. At night, he could be heard laughing and conversing with the guards and soldiers. It was rare when a Filipino collaborated with the Japanese, and the other natives in the area hated the ugly little man. Mac thought they hated him even more than the prisoners did. He would play an even bigger part in the lives of the Palawan POWs in the months to come.

It was October 19, 1944, shortly after the prisoners had returned to the barracks. Tired and dirty as always, Mac was getting ready for his half-mess kit of rice when he heard a strange noise in the distance. At first, the sound didn't register, but as it grew louder, he realized he'd never heard a sound quite like it. By now, he recognized the sounds made by Japanese Betty Bombers and Zeros, but not this sound. It was a low, powerful rumble. As Mac and Smitty wiped the grime off their bodies, the sound became louder, and they looked at one another for an answer. Then they looked out to the bay, where they saw a lone four-engine plane coming out of the clouds, skimming low over the water toward the prison camp. Neither had ever seen a plane quite like it. It had a twin tail; its overhead wing and bulky body bristled with bombs and machine guns. The ground shook as the bomber hedge-hopped over the camp and, for the first time in a long, long time, Mac and Smitty saw the Stars and Stripes on a plane's wings.

Both of them went crazy—whooping, yelling, screaming, dancing and jumping with joy—and they weren't alone. Every prisoner in the camp went wild. Their pith helmets, creased and recreased by the blows of Japanese clubs, went flying in the air. Every prisoner broke down emotionally, some of them crying. Others laughed as the plane rumbled over the camp, the pilot flapping his wings in greeting to the POWs below. As he roared across the camp, he picked up altitude and went to work. His first target was the docks, where two small ships and six Japanese seaplanes went up in flames. Not yet content, the pilot turned, circled and lined up on the just-completed airfield. His bombing was precise. He plopped three two-thousand pound bombs, one … two … three, right down the middle of the runway. Now, no Japanese Zeros could land on the concrete until the prisoners had filled in the holes.

After dropping the bombs, the huge plane circled back over the prison camp for a second time and flapped its wings, indicating to Mac that the pilot and crew would be returning. It was a glorious day for the Palawan prisoners, who had, for the first time in nearly three years, something to cheer about. When the bomber was out of sight, Mac, Smitty and the others looked around the prison and discovered there were no guards, no soldiers anywhere in sight. The Japanese had found holes to crawl into, but it didn't take long after the attack for them to crawl out of their bomb shelters and rush into the compound. They brought their clubs with them and spent the early evening hours beating the prisoners. Mac didn't care, and he took the beatings without a whimper. He knew the club swinging would soon be coming to an end.

From that day, there wasn't a day the Palawan prisoners didn't see an American bomber. Mac was told by a Japanese guard that the plane was a B-24 Liberator. The B-24, with its long range and ability to carry 16,000 pounds of high explosives—one 4,000-pound bomb on each wing and four 2,000-pound bombs in its belly—would soon replace all the B-17s in the Pacific War. The B-24s would return to Palawan again and again, flying out of range of Japanese antiaircraft guns. Every day at noon, the prisoners could count on the Liberator they called "Hysterical Harry." He was given the name because the Japanese ran like madmen to their bomb shelters when he was spotted. Harry flew over daily, dropped a few bombs, strafed aircraft on the ground, and flew away. He never missed a day.

The bombing raids were devastating. October 28 saw the destruction of at least sixty Japanese Zeros parked along the runway. In all, there had been about 150 planes hidden in the jungle, protected by the revetments the prisoners had been forced to build. The raids put the airfield out of commission until the prisoners could fill in the craters.

With the daily noontime appearance of Harry, and the regular appearance of flights of bombers over the airfield and docks, the guards took out their frustration on the prisoners. Beatings increased, and they

With antiaircraft shells bursting beneath the belly of "Hysterical Harry," the big bomber drops its payload on the recently completed airfield (U.S. War Department).

were harsh—no simple whack on the top of a man's pith helmet with one of their clubs. Now, they'd use any type of club to bring down a prisoner. Deguchi was good at this. Watching Mac and his crew filling in bomb craters, Deguchi grabbed a pick handle, and for no reason walked over to prisoner John Stanley and clubbed him on the head. Stanley, who wasn't wearing any type of head gear, dropped to the ground unconscious, a huge gash on his head. There was no reason for the clubbing. It was just something Deguchi wanted to do.

The POWs asked permission to paint "American Prisoner of War Camp" on the roof of the barracks. At first the Japanese refused, but then relented. The sign was painted on the roof. This gave the POWs some measure of comfort, and the Japanese took advantage of it by storing some of their supplies under the POW barracks.

It was all so innocent, a conversation Mac heard taking place between two of the Japanese guards. He understood enough Japanese by now to know what they were saying, and didn't have to spend a lot of time piecing it together. The guards were talking about Italy surrendering and that Germany was about to quit the war. In the retelling, the young Marine added a bit more to the story, in hopes of boosting morale in the camp. He told almost all the prisoners in the barracks about Germany and Italy, then innocently added that Japan would be the next country to surrender. Nothing evil about Mac's intentions—just a morale booster—but the Japanese found out. Mac believed Pedro Pajie, the Filipino scout turned traitor, somehow found out he'd been spreading the rumors around the camp and told the guards. Reaction was immediate. They came into the compound, grabbed Mac and dragged him to the camp brig. He yelled at them that it was all a joke, that he did it to keep up morale in the camp, but the guards believed he'd been in contact with a Filipino spy, and they wanted to know his name.

Once in the brig, the guards told Mac they were going to beat a confession out of him, and they didn't waste time. They tied his hands behind his back and then hung him from the rafters. The guards took turns beating him, and when they tired of the strap, they used their yard-long sticks. The beating lasted the rest of the afternoon and into the night, but Mac didn't give in and stuck to his story. Bloodied and bruised, the Iowa Marine finally convinced the interpreter it was all a joke, and when the interpreter managed to convince the guards that Mac had only been joking, they cut him down from the rafters. He fell to the floor. Mac lay there for a few minutes trying to regain his senses and, finally, managed to get up on all fours and to his feet. As he stood there shaking his head and trying to regain some sense of what had happened, Lieutenant Toru Ogawa, a short, heavyset and thick-necked man who looked like a Sumo wrestler, walked into the room. Ogawa walked over to Mac and said, "Huh, some joke!" Mac didn't see it coming. Ogawa's fist lashed out, hitting Mac squarely on the jaw and knocking him backwards over the table and chairs in the room. He was out cold again. When he regained his senses for the second time that day, they dragged him back to the barracks, dumped him on the floor and walked away, as if nothing had happened. But Smitty, who had thought he'd never see his buddy again, was overjoyed at his return and helped him to his sleeping mat.

9

Air Raid Shelters

It was November, and for about a month Hysterical Harry had been driving the Japanese nuts. They could count on the single flyover every day, and he always left a calling card of bombs and .50-caliber bullets. In one low pass over the prison camp, one of Harry's waste gunners pitched out handfuls of spent cartridges to the prisoners below—little mementos. And if Harry wasn't overhead, the Japanese knew they could expect much larger air strikes.

It was a typical November day for that part of the world. It hadn't rained for some time, skies were clear, and it was hot. Mac was helping fill craters on the runway when he looked out over the Sulu Sea. It was a sight to behold. He counted seven waves of seven bombers each flying in low over the Sea. All of them, it seemed, were flying right toward him. Mac wasn't the only one that made a mad scramble to the jungle. The bombers made quick work of the airfield and then swung around and concentrated on the ships in the harbor. Not a bomb fell on the prison camp or the Catholic Church in Puerto Princesa—at least not yet.

Filling the bomb craters which pocked all three runways was becoming routine. They ran for cover while American B-24s created more work for them. They didn't mind the interruptions, and only one prisoner was injured during all the bombings. Sergeant James Stidham from Hardshell, Kentucky, was hit by a rock blasted out of the ground by the bombing. It was a serious wound. Besides the large gash on his head, Stidham had a brain injury, which paralyzed him. Doc Mango did all he could to help—massaging and exercising his arms and legs—but he had no medicines of any kind and only a bit of gauze. Nothing worked, and Stidham lay on a stretcher staring at the ceiling through crossed eyes for days on end.

Enemy antiaircraft shells hardly ever reached high enough to bring down the U.S. bombers and fighters that plagued the Japanese below (U.S. War Department).

With American bombs creeping closer to Puerto Princesa and the prison camp, the prisoners were told to dig bomb shelters inside the prison barbed wire. They dug three big bomb shelters and smaller two- and three-man shelters, which were scattered about the prison compound. The big trenches were five feet deep and four feet wide, and one of them, Shelter A, was long enough to hold up to fifty men. Shelter B, just north of the main building, held about 35 prisoners. Shelter C, west of the main building, ended beneath the barbed wire at cliff's edge, above the seashore. It had room enough for 25 to 30 men. This was the trench Mac and Smitty helped dig and took refuge in during the bombings. All of them, Mac included, tried to convince the guards that a second entrance to the tunnel was needed, in case a direct hit sealed off the opening, but the guards wouldn't hear of it. When they had completed the digging, the prisoners placed coconut tree logs and old boards over the top and added a hefty layer of dirt to cushion the impact of a near hit. Mac and Smitty gave a lot of thought to the location of the shelter, and they dug it close to the cliff, which dropped down to the bay. They'd decided early on there would be two exits—to hell with what the guards wanted—and they dug it long enough that only about six inches of earth, hidden by a rock they'd placed at the end, separated them from breaking out and falling or rolling down the 60-foot incline to the shoreline and a chance at freedom. The hidden tunnel exit extended beyond the barbed wire fence that surrounded the prison compound. If need be, they had a clear shot at getting down the cliff.

The Palawan prisoners always knew when it was noon. Like so many factory whistles which sounded at noon in hundreds of towns across America, Hysterical Harry could always be counted on to let them know what time it was. He dropped out of his safe zone at 28,000 feet, got low enough to give the prisoners some additional work on the runways, then placed the rest of his payload on any available targets in the bay. Not content with the noon flyover, Harry started returning late at night, usually about midnight, to drop a few more bombs on the airfield.

On still another sunny November day, Mac watched as a half-dozen Zero fighter planes took off before noon and gained altitude. Once up to their operational limit, they waited for Harry to drop down from his perch. Although it looked like an ambush, the Iowa Marine was about to see a dogfight, and a one-sided one at that.

The Zeros circled the airfield waiting for Harry to show up, and he didn't disappoint them. As he dropped down to attack level, three of the Zeros pounced. It was Harry's lucky day. The B-24 had ten .50-caliber machine guns on board—twin .50s in the nose, tail, on top and in the belly, and two single machine guns on the sides. It was a formidable killing machine. As Mac's Japanese guards watched and screamed, "Banzai! Banzai!" three of the Zeros were shot out of the sky. The other three high-tailed it for the field. Harry gave his usual salute by dipping each wing—first the left and then the right—as he headed for home. Mac tried to hide his glee. If he didn't, he'd be pounded to the ground again by a guard's club.

Army Staff Sergeant Joseph Uballe, who was from Boone, Iowa, just up the road from Mac's hometown of Urbandale, watched as two of the Zeros landed without incident. The third came in at full speed. The pilot didn't let up on the throttle fast enough, and the fighter plane ran off the runway into the trees. As he climbed out of the cockpit and walked away, he looked over at Uballe and Mac and, in almost perfect English, said, "I feel a hell of a lot safer down here!"

Mac and Uballe stood there silently, looking at the fighter plane. Uballe was a small, quiet man who never said much. In the years they'd been POWs, Mac had never heard him say a word. But that day, Uballe looked up at him and said, "Do you think we could get in that plane and take off?" Surprised at the question and who it came from, Mac said, "Yea, I suppose we could. I don't know how to fly. Do you?" Staring longingly at the fighter, Uballe answered with a quiet, "I could certainly try." Mac paused, thought a moment and then said, "Don't you think we would get shot down by our own planes?" Uballe looked up at Mac. A smile spread across his face, and with a chuckle he said, "I never thought of that. Well, it was a hell of an idea!" They both went back to work filling bomb craters.

In addition to the B-24s, high-tailed B-17s, not yet taken out of action in the Pacific, became part of the formations which visited Palawan almost every day. Mac and Smitty soon saw an American fighter plane they'd never seen before, the formidable, twin-tailed P-38 Air Cobra, which also made daily flights over the island. The daily visits by heavy bombers, and now fighter planes, were a tell-tale sign that soon American troops would liberate the island, ending the beatings and torture the prisoners had endured for nearly two and a half years. Mac, Smitty and the other prisoners of Palawan would go home.

Negros, Philippine Islands

Lieutenant General Seiichi Terada, Commander of the 2nd Air Division, 4th Air Army, commanded all air units and air tactics in the Philippines from his headquarters on Negros, a boot-shaped island southeast of Palawan. It wasn't quite as far from Puerto Princesa as was Manila, but was still far enough away that Terada knew little about the 131st Airfield Battalion on Palawan, which had been transferred to his command by the 4th Air Army commander, General Tominaga. Terada didn't want command of the battalion, but he was stuck with it. On December 9, 1944, he would discuss that and other problems throughout the day with General Tominaga's Chief of Staff, Major General Kumabe.

On December 10, a Japanese lookout post at Surigao, on the northern tip of Mindanao, spotted an American convoy of 300–400 ships heading General Terada's way. The next day, General Terada sent out two reconnaissance planes. They reported the huge convoy of troop transports, battleships and aircraft carriers heading west toward a possible landing on Negros Island. Word was flashed to Manila, Palawan and all other

Japanese bases in the Philippines. However, Terada still wasn't sure where the convoy was heading, and he suspected the Americans were making a feint to draw attention away from their main target. He sent out another reconnaissance flight the next day. It reported no change in the American convoy's speed or direction. Their target still appeared to be Negros Island.

Terada was still unconvinced, and, taking no chances, he sent out more reconnaissance flights. This time, the direction of the convoy indicated it had changed its course and was moving northwest in the Sulu Sea. That was all the information General Terada needed. He believed the American armada was heading for Palawan. He sent this message to all units: "As a result of this morning's reconnaissance, the enemy fleet is sailing northwest on the Sulu Sea. Division will now divert strength from the Leyte area and concentrate on the enemy fleet. Probable landing on Palawan Island expected."

Palawan, Philippine Islands, December 12, 1944

Mac and Smitty could feel the tension and pent-up anger of the guards who watched over them as they worked at patching holes in the runway. They knew enough Japanese, and had picked up on enough of the talk between the guards, to know that an American task force was headed their way. There wasn't a prisoner in camp who didn't know that something big was happening beyond Palawan. Meanwhile, the prisoners continued their regular routine of working with wheelbarrows and shovels, filling the craters and repaving blown out sections of the airstrip, and stopping to dash for the jungle when more American bombers showed up to blow new holes in the runway. There were also times the Japanese kept the prisoners out in the open, hoping the bombardiers above would take notice and drop their payload away from the runway.

The nearly 400-ship American convoy was just south of the Cuyo Islands when General Terada received a top secret dispatch from the 131st Battalion Commander on Palawan requesting advice and instructions on a "certain matter." The wireless arrived while Terada was conferring with General Kumabe, an aide to General Tominaga, about operational procedure during an American invasion and about who had jurisdiction over the Palawan battalion. The message read, in part, "The natives in the vicinity of the airfield hold a hostile attitude. From time to time, they have been attacking the airfield. All those harboring an enemy feeling we will wipe out and maintain the airfield. Request advice as to action to take regarding the POWs at the time of the enemy landing."

General Terada thought about it. He later summarized his thoughts this way: "Since a smaller unit was facing a problem and requesting instruction from a higher command during an emergency, it was only right that I should do something, despite the fact I had no jurisdiction over the Palawan airfield battalion, but that problem would be ironed out later." Terada discussed the matter with General Kumabe and then sent off a dispatch to 4th Army Commander, General Tominaga. They received his reply in the early evening. Acting on General Tominaga's dispatch, General Terada drafted the following reply to Palawan: "Jurisdiction over your unit is presently being investigated by the Army Chief of Staff and 2nd Air Division. In reference to your wireless request: (1) Pertaining to wiping out the natives, carry on as you see fit. (2) At the time of the enemy landing, if the POWs are harboring an enemy feeling, dispose of them at the appropriate time. The above mentioned lines of action are based on an army order. Signed: 2nd Air Division Commander." The order to execute was sent immediately after it was drafted—150 American slave laborers had just been sentenced to death. General Terada thought no more about it. There were more important things to think about.

While Mac and Smitty toiled away on the airfield on December 13, some of their comrades in Manila Harbor were dying. Over 1,600 POWs were crammed so tightly into the hold of a Japanese ship that some men went berserk killing each other, while others died of suffocation. One of those men who suffocated in the Japanese transport was Mac's commanding officer of the 3rd Battalion, 4th Marines, Lieutenant Colonel John P. Adams. U.S. Navy planes bombed the Japanese convoy, and the ship limped into Subic Bay, but not before 419 POWs were killed by suffocation, bombing or drowning while attempting to swim to shore.

Captain Kojima, the 131st Airfield Battalion Commander on Palawan received the top-secret message from General Terada in late evening on December 13. After reading it, he assembled his staff, Lieutenants Ozawa, Yoshirwara, Chino, Yamamoto, Abe and Ogawa. There was little time to spare. They all thought the huge American invasion force was headed right for them. The plan was simple enough: Cover all the escape routes, set up fields of fire and crossfire so the prisoners had no chance of making a run for it, and have a gun barge patrolling the waters off the beach below the Puerto Princesa prison camp. The prisoners were to die by fire, hand grenade, rifle and machine gun fire, bayoneting and clubbing.

With no time to waste, all members of the 131st Airfield Battalion were called out shortly after midnight and sent to the airfield to repair any damage that had been done from earlier bombings. Meanwhile, Urbandale's Glenn McDole, his best buddy from Texas, Rufus Smith, and the rest of the POW's slept soundly in their barracks. That is, they slept soundly until around two o'clock in the morning of December 14, when guards entered the building, rousted them out and headed them to the airfield to make all necessary repairs. Stumbling out of the barracks half asleep, Mac realized he hadn't been called out of the rack that early since a little more than three years before, when the Japs had bombed Pearl Harbor. They'd put in a hard day's work the previous day and were exhausted, but they moved out of the barracks and headed toward the airfield.

They were at work well before sunrise, and with first light, the prisoners noticed there were more soldiers guarding them than usual. Gun crews were on station at all the big guns along the runway, their barrels pointed out to sea. Smitty stopped work for a moment, leaned on his shovel and said, "Somethin's goin' on, Dole. What the hell do ya think is happening?" Mac had noticed the guards seemed anxious and nervous. He paused for a moment, shook his head, looked at Smitty and said, "God, I don't know! Maybe Uncle Sam is putting so much heat on 'em, they know we'll be freed soon." Both of them could feel the tension, and every prisoner on the field that day felt something big was about to happen. But their spirits were up. The Americans were coming, and all of them had one overriding thought—walking out of the main gate of the camp a free man and sailing home to America.

At eleven o'clock that morning, The Buzzard, Lieutenant Sato, arrived at the airfield carrying his little standing box. The guards pushed and prodded all the prisoners together while Sato whispered something to one of the guards. Then he placed the box on the ground, stood on it and announced, "Americans, your working days are over!" That was all he said. He stepped off the box as the guards began herding the prisoners back to the compound. Mac did his best to mask his feelings, because any outward sign of jubilation would bring a club or rifle butt down on his head. He and all the others believed the American invasion was now only hours away. Lieutenant Sato was right. Their working days had ended, and most of them would never see another sunrise.

10

The False Air Raid

When they walked through the main gate at midday, there were more guards than usual inside the compound, but they didn't think too much of it. They figured that, with Americans on the way, security had been beefed up. Most of them never for a moment thought the Japanese would kill them, but the thought did occur to Sergeant Douglas Bogue. He had been told by a Japanese guard that all the Americans would be killed if American troops landed on Palawan. Other POWs had ignored that statement. Bogue believed it.

Once inside the compound, Smitty suggested they sneak into the barracks and grab some papayas they had concealed from the guards. Both were hungry, and it took no coaxing on Smitty's part to get Mac into the barracks. No sooner had they entered the building than the low moan of the air raid siren sounded, its pitch rising higher and higher as guards with rifles entered the barracks and started pushing and hitting the prisoners to get them into the bomb shelters, screaming at them to take cover. Both Mac and Smitty made a beeline for Shelter C. They jumped in and waited. And waited. The siren continued for a while. Then it was quiet. There were reports of two P-38s overhead. Once they had left the area, the prisoners crawled out of their bunkers. They were all told to remain near their shelters, because there were supposedly hundreds of U.S. bombers on the way. They all stayed in the immediate area of their bomb shelters until about two o'clock, when the air-raid sirens sounded again and the guards screamed that hundreds of planes were headed toward Puerto Princesa. They all jumped back into their bunkers and waited for the bombs to fall. But none fell.

Like so many of his comrades in arms, Superior Private Tomisaburo

What remained of one of the bomb shelters (B shelter) inside the prison camp. The charred bones and ashes of the slaughtered prisoners can be seen at the bottom of the trench (U.S. War Department).

Sawa was a sadistic, brutal man. As a member of the 2nd Platoon, 131st Airfield Battalion, Sawa helped maintain the airfield and guarded the surrounding area. When half of Palawan's POWs were returned to Manila, Sawa stood guard over the remaining prisoners. He enjoyed his work. He was particularly fond of beating the prisoners with anything he could get his hands on. When nothing else could be found, he used his bare hands, but most of the time he used his rifle butt to knock a prisoner to the ground. Once he got them on their backs, he used his bayonet to cut them. He was choosy when it came to cutting. He always chose the men whose skin was softer due to dietary deficiencies.

It was noon, December 14th, when Sawa and the other soldiers making up the 2nd Platoon were told by their leader, W. O. Yamamoto, that the prisoners were to be killed and that they would take part in the massacre. Sawa and the others grabbed their rifles, fixed bayonets and were quickly loaded aboard a truck for the short ride to the POW camp. They formed up outside the prison's main gate and were given their killing orders by the man the POWs called "The Weasel," Captain Kojima. Each man was assigned a position inside the prison. Sawa was to take a guard position just a few feet from a machine gun on the prison veranda, near the stairway which led to the latrine. Their job was to kill any prisoner who attempted to evacuate the bomb shelters. The soldiers waited for orders to enter the prison and take their positions.

Through the prison's main gate came the 1st and 2nd platoons and a few men from the 3rd platoon of the 2nd Air Division. They knew what was expected of them. All of them were armed with rifles and bayonets, and some had hand grenades. Each man carried thirty rounds of ammunition, presumably enough to get the job done. Still other soldiers, the primary executioners, entered the compound with buckets of gasoline and torches. Armed soldiers were spaced about ten feet apart along the veranda, where a machine gun had been positioned. With all the guns set up to provide blanket coverage of the prison yard, there appeared to be no escape, no chance of surviving. There were at least seventy soldiers, maybe more, waiting on the killing field, December 14, 1944. The sun was high in the sky, and the slaughter was about to begin.

It was quiet in the bomb shelters. The prisoners waited. The air raid sirens had been quiet for some time, and as yet there was no sound of U.S. aircraft overhead. It was around 2:30 p.m. and, with about 30 men crammed into Mac and Smitty's bunker, they were becoming more agitated with every passing minute. It was hot and stuffy inside the shelters, and as they waited, prisoners in all the bomb shelters began complaining and yelling at the guards. The guards yelled back, telling them to stay where they were and not to look out of the shelter entrances. Still no sound of aircraft overhead, and some of the men began to realize that something bad—really bad—was about to happen.

Smitty told Mac, "Look out, Dole, and see if ya can see anything goin' on." Mac looked out the opening of the trench and saw soldiers entering the camp, dressed in full battle gear and carrying lighted torches, buckets of gas and rifles. He watched as the soldiers poured the gasoline down the only entrance to Shelter B. The torch went in, and there was a muffled "WHUMP!" as the gas exploded. Then came the agonizing screams from those trapped inside. Mac ducked back into the shelter and told everyone what he'd seen. Smitty decided to look out the opening, and a rifle shot forced him to duck back into the bunker. He had seen enough. "They're murdering the men in B-company pit!" he screamed. "Finish diggin' the tunnel!" There was a frenzied scramble to claw their way out of the shelter. It wouldn't take long to push out the six inches of dirt and move the rock aside. Shelter C was last on the list for extermination, so they had a little more time.

By now, the guards were rushing toward all the trenches with buckets of gasoline and torches. Rifle fire and short bursts from the machine guns were coming from every direction. Superior Private Sawa, with a clear view from the veranda, fired at three POWs who had crawled out of their bunkers. He dropped all three of them. Later, Sawa wasn't sure he'd been the actual killer, because there were so many other guards also firing at the prisoners.

The camp's beloved Doctor Carl Mango, who shared his small bomb shelter with Captain Bruni, Doctor Knight and Warrant Officer Glenn Turner, jumped from his shelter. He was covered with flames and fire as he ran toward the guards, waving his arms and pleading with them to stop the killing. The beloved doctor was cut down by gun fire as he made a final pleading gesture. Captain Sato, the camp's commandant, walked over to Mango, doused him with more gasoline and set him afire. The madness continued, with soldiers laughing and screaming as they fired away at POWs who made a desperate attempt to get out of their burning underground coffins.

Doug Bogue watched as a prisoner, engulfed in flames, rushed a Japanese guard, grabbed his rifle and shot him. He saw another guard bayonet a prisoner in the back. Bogue knew that if he were to survive, he'd have to make a run for it from his three-man shelter and slash his way through the barbed wire enclosure. Others had tried and failed, shot by soldiers lining the barracks veranda, but he had nothing to lose. He made a frantic scramble to the wire.

A Time to Flee

Mac took another quick look outside his shelter and saw Corporal Robert Hubbard emerging from his bunker in a sea of flames. A quick

The barrack's veranda where Japanese riflemen and a machine gunner were in position for the afternoon slaughter of 139 prisoners of war (U.S. War Department).

burst from a machine gun ended the Reno, Nevada, Marine's agony. Inside Shelter C, which stretched beyond the barbed wire, the prisoners continued digging furiously as those inside, some of whom had never been in that shelter, were screaming and yelling encouragement. As yet, no attack on Shelter C had been made, only sporadic rifle fire aimed at keeping the prisoners inside. But Mac did manage to see some of the carnage taking place above-ground. He spotted nine POWs (Doug Bogue, Fern Barta, Edwin Petry, Donald Martyn, Alberto Pacheco, Doug Burnett and Jesse Simpson, plus two others he didn't recognize) crawling furiously toward the barbed wire. Others in the prison yard were making the same attempt. Some of these men died from rifle fire, and some were to die later, but the nine men who plunged through the wire with Doug Bogue made it down the cliff. Bogue found his way to a small depression between two rocks. His body cut by the barbed wire and his feet slashed and bloody from the coral, he waited.

Eugene Nielsen of Logan, Utah, was right behind Bogue and the others, and he headed for the only place he thought would save him from being shot and burned—the camp's garbage dump. He dug a hole in it, covering himself with garbage and coconut husks, and waited.

Navy Radioman 1st Class Fern Barta paused just long enough at the bottom of the cliff to apply a tourniquet to the arm of Dane Hamric, who had made it down the cliff but who was in a bad way, his arm nearly torn off by rifle fire. Barta ran on to find refuge on his own. He knew those who stood on the beach too long would be cut down. The guards hadn't yet come down to the beach. Barta took refuge in a sewer outlet, and would soon be joined by others.

On the beach, Edwin Petry looked frantically for a place to hide. He found what appeared to be a small cave at water's edge and hid there with Albert Pacheco. Petry could hear the shooting taking place on the beach as guards rousted out the prisoners from their hiding places.

Back in the prison yard, Captain Sato walked over to James Stidham, who had been paralyzed during a bombing, took out his pistol, placed the barrel to Stidham's head, and fired. No letup in the bloodletting. It was a field day for the guards and officers of the prison camp.

In Shelter C, the prisoners finally broke through the hole, and it was every man out and on his own as they fell and stumbled down the cliff. Mac and Smitty were among the last men out of the bunker. A bucket of gas had been thrown into the bunker entrance, soaking Navy Corpsman Everett Bancroft, Jr., of Canon City, Colorado. Some of the gas had splashed on Mac's backside as he ran from the entrance to the exit. When the torch was thrown into the shelter Bancroft burst into flames and fell to the floor. Mac's shorts, soaked with gasoline, were set afire. He ripped them off as he ran down the shelter to the hidden exit, right behind Smitty. There he stood for a moment—shoes lost somewhere in the mad scramble, no clothing, naked as he was the day he was born.

Just as Mac was about to take the wild plunge, he looked down to see Pop Danielson, paralyzed with fear and squatting on the shelter floor. He yelled, "Come on, Pop!" but Pop wouldn't move. Mac dragged him to the shelter exit and put his hands on Pop's butt, flipping him out of the hole, where he tumbled down the hill to the beach. Corporal McDole was right behind him, the last man out, his butt burned red and his feet cut and bleeding from the sharp coral as he frantically jumped, fell and stumbled to the beach below. Bancroft's agonizing screams followed him down the hill.

Smitty and Mac were at the bottom. They paused for just a moment, looking at each other, fearing they'd never see one another again. They shook hands, both reluctant to release their grip, but they were losing precious time. Mac whispered, "This is it buddy, isn't it?" Smitty took one last look at him and said, "Yep, Dole. I'll be seein' ya!" They started running. Smitty's legs were longer, and he was faster. The distance between them widened as they ran down the beach. Suddenly, rifle fire began cutting into the prisoners who'd made it to the beach. A rifle shot hit near Mac, sending bits of coral into his right leg, but he hardly noticed as he took cover. Smitty, who had made it through the rifle fire, headed into a small ravine partway up the cliff and hunkered down to avoid the fire which came from the cliff above. One by one, the survivors on the beach were being picked off as they looked frantically for holes and caves.

In the compound, the killing continued, while those on the beach, too confused and disoriented to take cover, were being picked off by sharp-shooters. Although no one counted, it's believed that 30 to 40 POWs made it to the beach. Many were scrunched down in any hole or outcropping they could find. It was not the time to try swimming across the bay. The sun was high in the sky, and they'd soon be spotted by riflemen from the barge. Those who had made it down the cliff and entered the water during the height of the carnage began floating ashore by late afternoon.

Finding Refuge

Mac was on the beach and happily surprised to see so many of his friends had made it out of the killing field above. He had to find refuge, a safe place where the Japs wouldn't think a man could hide, and it didn't take him long to find it. He headed right for it, the prison camp's garbage dump, the huge pile of garbage and refuse which had been growing higher and higher during his years in captivity. The smell nearly suffocated Mac as he dived into what was normally home for the island's vermin. Ordinarily, just a whiff of the dump would cause a man to gag, but there was little time to spare, and Mac started digging into it, making a safe haven below the surface. He dug deeper and deeper into the garbage, doing his best to ignore the overpowering stench. At times he almost vomited, but he knew it was not the time to get sick. He dug deep, crawled down into it belly first and pulled garbage over the top of him. He could hardly breathe as the worms, maggots and other creatures in the dump found him and started making a home for themselves. He did not move.

He lay there, trying to figure out what his next move would be, when he felt and then heard someone digging into the garbage. It was Corporals Charles Street and Erving Evans, who were digging frantically to find refuge. By now, the guards were on the beach en force, and Mac could hear them talking. Then the shooting began, as they found prisoners among the rocks and in the small coral caves. Street couldn't take it any longer. He panicked and jumped up, running for the water. There was the crack of a rifle and the young corporal from Santa Cruz, California, died just short of water's edge. Mac and Evans stayed right where they were, both too frightened to talk, as the worms and other creatures began working on them, driving them crazy. Evans kept squirming and Mac whispered, "Quit moving, damnit! They're going to see us in here!" It was Evans' turn. He couldn't take it any longer, and he stood up shouting, "All right you Jap bastards, here I am and don't miss me you sons of bitches!" Another rifle shot and Corporal Evans, of Huron, South Dakota, fell dead on top of Mac, his body packing the garbage so tight that Mac almost couldn't breathe. He could feel the pressure of a guard's feet as he walked on top of him, and then felt the weight being taken off when Evan's body was pulled off the pile to a nearby tree. It was then he smelled the familiar odor of gasoline as they doused Evan's body and set him afire.

Mac wanted to run, but something kept telling him to stay put. He did, all the while praying to God to give him the strength to survive. As he prayed, he could hear the laughter of the guards and smell the stench of burning flesh. The odor of flesh burning and garbage was overwhelming, but he managed again to fight off a powerful urge to vomit. There were other sounds along the beach: screams of other POWs as they were bayoneted, burned, beaten and shot, then the laughter of the guards as they set fire to the living and the dead. Then it was quiet, very quiet. The killing on the beach had lasted about an hour. By then, the Japanese believed they had killed all the POWs, but there would be another body count and another search.

Back in the prison yard, the leader of the 2nd platoon, W. O. Yamamoto, walked over to a prisoner not yet dead, lying face down. Yamamoto unsheathed his sword, raised it above his head and brought it down on the back of the prisoner's neck, beheading him.

It was quiet when Mac decided to take a look outside. He made a small opening and fresh air seeped in, but he closed it up again. About 25 yards from his hole in the garbage stood six guards who had surrounded a prisoner. They prodded him with their bayonets, making small cuts on his body. Another guard, carrying a bucket of gasoline and a torch joined them as they continued poking him with their bayonets. Mac watched as the American pleaded with the guards not to burn him. "Please shoot me, please don't burn me! I don't want to burn!" he screamed. The guards laughed at him as he screamed, "Shoot me you bastards! You stupid sons of bitches, shoot me!"

They doused his left foot first and set it afire. His screaming continued as they set his right foot afire. Then they doused gasoline on his hands as he screamed, "Oh God! Please! Please!" He collapsed on the sand. With that, the guards soaked his whole body with gasoline. When the flames died down, they dragged the body to a nearby tree, where they used it for bayonet practice. Mac got sick, quietly. Real sick. Sick of it all.

While Mac was buried in the garbage dump, Smitty had made it up the ravine and into the jungle which surrounded the prison camp. He was no more than 10 yards from the barbed wire, where the foliage and weeds were so thick that a Japanese guard, standing at the edge of the wire, looked right at him but couldn't see him. From his vantage point, he saw it all: the continued shooting and burning of the prisoners, the beheadings, POWs screaming and begging to be put out of their misery. Years later, Smitty still remembered the laughter among the guards as they continued the slaughter. He watched as the bodies of the POWs were partially covered with dirt in their bomb shelters, and then dynamited to make it appear that their deaths were caused by American bombers. He listened to the chatter of the officers and guards in the camp as they went about the grim task of dynamiting the dead. He heard one officer say a body count showed 149 prisoners were killed. Smitty was stunned. As far as he knew, he was the only survivor, and he knew they'd come looking for him. He slowly backed away from the prison camp and found the little weed-packed depression he'd sought safety in during the massacre. Then, he heard the guards moving through the jungle looking for those who might have escaped. He did not move. The weeds and the jungle foliage were so thick a Japanese guard walking through the depression stepped on him, but kept on walking. By this time, the lanky Texan was so tired and traumatized by the slaughter that he could hardly move. He'd wait until dark to make his escape. He lay there in the undergrowth and went to sleep.

By now, the guards were scouring the beach for more survivors. Eugene Nielsen, from Logan, Utah, buried in the garbage, could hear the screams of the POWs on the beach as they were targeted for burning and bayoneting. The guards decided to make another search of the garbage pile, and one of them stepped on Nielsen, looked down at him, removed a few coconut husks from Neilsen's back, and told the other guards there was another dead body in the garbage pile. Just as he was about to drag Nielsen from the pile, he was ordered back up the cliff. It was time to eat.

When the guard walked away, Nielsen got up and started running down the beach. He ran into a cove where, to his delight, he found about 15 other POWs. His joy was short-lived. A gun barge appeared offshore and opened fire. Nielsen saw about eight of his comrades killed by rifle and machine gun fire.

There was no time to lose. The former coastal artilleryman on Corregidor dove into the water and started swimming. Guards were approaching the cove from both sides, and he was swimming parallel to the shoreline. The guards on shore were firing at him as they walked down the beach. Rufus Smith, who watched it all from the cliff above before he took cover in the dense jungle brush, told Nielsen years later that the Japs, about 10 of them, must have fired close to a hundred shots at him, because they emptied their rifles and reloaded, only to reload again. Nielsen kept swimming and submerging to escape the rifle fire, which pocked the water around him. One bullet had already struck him in the leg, but it didn't slow him down. Another shot grazed his head, and still another grazed his ribs and arm, but he kept swimming as the current swept him further into the bay. Near exhaustion, he kept at it and, finally, his feet touched bottom. He staggered to shore. With what little energy he had left, he scurried to the protection of the jungle and sought concealment in a mangrove swamp. He submerged what part of his body he could in the mud and waited as the mosquitoes and other curious animals and vermin of the swamp moved in to make a home for themselves. Not too long after his swim and his stay in the swamp, he was discovered by friendly Filipinos, and he began his long trip south to Brookes Point at the southern end of Palawan, where his wounds were treated. They never found the bullet that had entered his leg as he swam out into the bay.

Mac was now the only man left in the garbage pile, and he stayed there through the night. He tried to sleep, but couldn't. And he did not move.

When it was dark, Rufus Smith moved slowly and cautiously through the jungle and down to the beach. Smitty spotted a guard nearby and waited until he turned away. He then eased himself into the water, knowing the tide would erase his bloody footprints from the coral. He started swimming the five to seven miles across the bay. Just offshore, he removed his tattered canvas shorts to cut down on drag. The tide kept pushing him further out into the bay than he wanted to go. As he struggled to make a correction, he lost sight of the shoreline and became frightened. But, compared to what was about to happen, losing sight of land was a small matter. He saw a shark's fin cutting through the water toward him. He swam faster, trying to outrun it, but it was no contest. He thrashed about trying to scare it off, but the shark bit down hard on his arm, and he could feel the teeth sinking into him as it tore away pieces of his flesh. Luck was with him the night of December 14. Just when he thought he'd reached the end, he spotted more fins coming toward him. They were not sharks. A school of dolphins moved quickly through the water to his rescue. They drove off the shark, and, as he swam, they kept a protective shield around him. He could hardly raise his arms to swim and tried to hitch a ride on one of the dolphins, but it wouldn't cooperate. They stayed with him through the night and escorted him to within sight of the shoreline.

Smitty, like all the others who would make the swim to freedom, was exhausted. He was close to land but still in deep water. He spotted a fish net. He grabbed one of the poles and hung on, trying to regain some strength. Just as he grabbed the pole, a Japanese patrol boat appeared out of nowhere, and he pulled himself beneath the surface until the boat had passed. When he surfaced, the boat was gone. He'd managed to elude them again. His feet still could not touch bottom, and as tired as he was, he made a few strokes toward shore, but started sinking. His knees touched bottom. Using the last bit of strength remaining, he kept his knees moving forward until his head came out of the water. From there it was an agonizing crawl to the beach. It was still dark, and Smitty lay at water's edge for about two hours. The two-hour rest helped. When dawn broke, he knew he'd have to put as much distance as possible between himself and the Japanese. He could see the huts of the Iwahig Penal Colony, but he wouldn't go there. Instead, he headed for a broad swamp and plunged into it. Driven nearly crazy by mosquitoes as he waded through knee-deep muck, Smitty covered his body with mud and moved through the swamp, jumping from one huge tree root to another. Naked, cut, shark-bitten and bruised, he made it through the mangrove swamp, found a wild pig trail and followed it.

Earlier on the day of the massacre, about mid-afternoon, Dane Hamrick had crawled into the cave where he found Edwin Petry and one other POW. Hamric was in great pain from the gunshot wound that had nearly severed his arm. He was half-crazed from the ordeal. He wouldn't shut up. Petry said later, "We had to slap him around a bit to keep him quiet, because guards were overhead looking for openings in the coral."

It was about five p.m. when Barta, Bogue, Martyn and Lyons entered the cave and told them the search on the beach had intensified and that there were barges offshore waiting to shoot any prisoner who tried swimming the bay. They had no alternative. They waited in the cave until nightfall. They were almost discovered. Lyons had a lung ailment and couldn't stop coughing. His coughing caught the attention of the prison guards above, but, unable to find any opening, they walked away.

About nine in the evening of December 14, Sergeant Doug Bogue of San Diego, California, Navy Radioman Fern Barta from Oregon, Marine Private First Class Donald Martyn of Hollywood, California, and Army Privates Edwin Petry of Santa Monica, California, and Alberto Pacheco of Deming, New Mexico, slipped into the water at about 15-yard intervals and started their swim to freedom. Dane Hamric was too weak to make the swim. All of them became separated during the night, and one of them, Donald Martyn, did not make it. He either drowned in the bay or died somewhere in the island's jungle. He was never seen again. The four who made it ashore landed at different locations. As for Doug Bogue, he made the shortest swim. Disoriented and with little energy, he ended up walking for five days and nights without water or food. He was rescued by Filipino prisoners at the Iwahig Penal Colony. They called in guerrilla fighters, who took him south to Brookes Point.

The night of December 14, there was still a lot of activity in the prison camp. The guards continued their search for POWs still believed to be on the beach or in the jungle. Two prisoners, William Balchus and Elmo Deal, had watched from the jungle when the Japanese were firing at Eugene Nielsen in the bay. As they moved out of the bush and down to the beach, they ran into two more prisoners. They talked about different avenues of escape but couldn't agree, so Balchus and Deal decided to make their escape through the jungle. It was pitch black when five guards headed down the cliff to the beach. Three of the guards carried torches, and Balchus and Deal had no alternative at this point. Balchus slammed a big hunk of coral into one of the guard's heads, and then the two men, according to Balchus, jumped the other two guards and killed them. At this point, Balchus decided to swim. Deal, who had a shoulder wound, climbed back up the cliff and made his way to freedom through the jungle. Both were found by friendly Filipinos and were later taken to the southern end of the island.

11

The Swim

The Japanese finally realized they had not killed all the POWs. The next morning, they began a methodical search of the beach, probing into all the cliff's small caves and holes along the shoreline. When the sun came up, Corporal Glenn McDole looked out on the beach from a very small peephole he'd made in the garbage. Suddenly, and without any warning, a Japanese soldier was on the pile, looking directly down at him. Mac thought he could smell the guard's breath and body odor, and he thought he'd soon feel the thrust of a bayonet. All he could think of was what they would do with him. What kind of torture would they put him through? If he ran, would he be able to dodge the bullets? He closed his eyes and did not move. He sought guidance, this time from a much higher power. It wasn't the first time he'd prayed during the years he'd spent in captivity, and he asked again for guidance and protection. When Mac opened his eyes, the guard was gone.

At that moment, a shot rang out down the beach, and the guards near the garbage pile ran toward the shooting, hoping to get in on the killing. With the guards out of sight, Mac stood up for the first time since he'd scurried down the cliff. He started running, and he ran north as fast as he could, in the opposite direction of the shooting. As he ran up the beach, he saw the bloated bodies of some of his comrades as the waves rocked them gently back and forth along the shoreline. He spotted a homemade bandage, which at one time had been used to protect the ulcer which was eating away at the leg of one of Doug Bogue's bunker mates. Mac couldn't remember his name, but he knew he had to be dead. The coral was shredding the bottoms of his feet, but he ran on. At this point he was oblivious to the pain. He knew he was leaving a blood trail, so he ran to the edge of the water and continued running until he tripped and fell. Lying there exhausted, he looked up to see what appeared to be a tunnel in the coral rocks. He ducked underwater and came up inside the cave, where there was just enough room for a couple of men to sit on a ledge with their feet in the water. It was a sewer outlet. It was very dark inside. As the waves hit the shoreline, a small stream of water trickled down on him. The small crabs who made their home in the cave began working on him. The cave's protection from bayonets, rifles and gasoline gave him no other choice. He'd tolerate the crabs.

As he sat there in the dark, all the killing and torture he'd been witness to returned, and he started shaking. He closed his eyes and tried to think of other things, pleasant times back home in Iowa, the good times in the Philippines before the war, but it didn't work. All he could see, all he could think of, was the burned, bayoneted and bullet-riddled bodies of his fellow prisoners. A chill swept through him. He wanted to vomit, but there was nothing in his stomach. He sat in that little cave, a cramp in his guts, and he suffered through the dry heaves.

At sunset on December 15, the guards left the beach, and Mac decided to make the swim across the bay. He hadn't been in the water long when a storm came up—high winds and waves—and he knew he couldn't make it across. Forced back to shore, he found another hiding place in the rocks and waited for the weather to improve. Just as he'd curled up to get some sleep, he heard someone splashing in the water. When Mac looked out, he saw a pair of legs. By the color of the skin and the bruises which covered the man's calves, he had to be an American. "Hey, American!" Mac whispered. The man bent down and began searching for the voice. "Where in hell are ya?" he said. Mac stuck his head out of the hole and recognized Dane Hamric, the soldier from Widen, West Virginia, who'd been shot early on in the massacre and had somehow managed to avoid capture. Hamric was in bad shape. His arm nearly shot off, Hamric had lost a tremendous amount of blood. Mac took a look at the wound. He could tell gangrene had set in. It would be only a matter of time, a short amount of time, before Hamric would die unless medical care was found. He washed Hamric's wound with saltwater, and although he was in a lot of pain, Hamric managed to tell Mac what he knew about the others who'd made a swim for freedom. Hamric rattled off the names and Mac listened, hoping that Smitty's name would come up, but it didn't. Mac thought he'd lost his buddy. They stayed in the sewer outlet throughout the day. There was no activity on the beach. Hamric grew weaker.

While Mac was tending to Hamric, Smitty had reached the edge of a mangrove swamp to the south and spotted native huts in the distance. Although he didn't know it at the time, it was a prison work farm. There were no guards, and the prisoners were on the honor system. As Smitty approached the nearest hut, dogs started barking, and one of the prisoners came down the path toward him. He grabbed the prisoner by the neck and told him he'd kill him if he made any false moves. The Filipino pleaded with Smitty, saying he was his friend, that he wouldn't turn him over to the Japanese. Smitty released the Filipino, who then ran to the prison farm for help, because the young Texan was drained of energy at this point. It was then that Smitty saw Pedro Pajie walking down the path toward him. Pajie was the Filipino turncoat who had appeared at the Palawan prison camp and spit on and taunted the American prisoners. When Pajie was close enough, Smitty, using what little energy remained, lunged for him. Pajie backed up and pulled his pistol from his holster. When Pajie saw who it was, he tossed his pistol to the now-dumbfounded former prisoner. Pajie said, "I know what you think, but I wasn't working for the Japanese. I was gathering information for the guerrillas." With that, Smitty collapsed. The Filipinos carried him back to their huts, cleaned him up, painted his scratched and bitten body with iodine and fitted him with clothes. He would be traveling south that night.

On the beach at Puerto Princesa, Mac and Hamrick had returned to the the sewer outlet. They decided to wait until the evening of the 16th before attempting a swim to freedom. Hamric was in a lot of pain and wasn't communicating very well. As they sat there, they heard the welcome sound of American bombers overhead. They didn't dare look out to see how many bombers were above them, but from the number of explosions, there had to be quite a few. The bombs shook the earth, and many of them fell closer to the prison camp than before. There was one tremendous explosion, and those natives who saw it later said they had never seen anything like it. Bombs had been dropped on the Catholic church in Puerto Princesa, and it went up like a gigantic Roman candle. The Japanese had stored all their ammunition and explosives in the church, and, apparently, Filipino guerrillas had sent this information on to American forces.

When General Homma's 14th Army had invaded the Philippines, the Japanese force had never achieved a complete conquest of the nation. The Japanese owned the cities and larger towns, as well as the vast, flat expanses of the island of Luzon where they could easily spot their enemy, but the guerrillas owned the jungles of the thousands of islands that made up the Philippines. They had continued to carry the war to the Japanese. America had promised the Philippines independence, and the Philippine people waited anxiously for the Americans to deliver on that promise.

When the sun went down on the evening of December 16, Mac made one more attempt to swim the bay. He tried to take Hamric with him. Hamric was very weak, and Mac knew he would have to tow the wounded man across the bay. He barely had the energy to swim across it alone, but he would try.

Almost as soon as they got into deep water, Hamric started resisting Mac's efforts to keep him afloat and moving. He thrashed about in the water and fought off Mac's efforts to keep him up. Mac felt they would both drown. It was then that the Iowa Marine decided to head back to shore to the safety of his small cave. He hit Hamric as hard as he could, knocking him out, and then towed him to shore, where they both settled into the sewer outlet. There they spent the next day, December 17.

Inside the coral outcropping that night, Mac washed Hamric's wound again, and noticed there was more bleeding. With the gangrene spreading through his body, Mac knew Hamric would die soon. Hamric looked up at Mac and moaned, "I can't make it Mac. You go on! You know I can't make it, so go on and get the hell out of here and let me die!" "Hang on, my friend, you'll be okay," Mac whispered. "You just hang on a while longer," Mac urged. "Do ya think I can make it, Mac?" Dane moaned. "You can make it," Mac whispered. "Come on buddy, you gotta stick it out with me! You can't leave me by myself. I need you!" After a while, there was little talk. Dane Hamric tried, but the infection and loss of blood was too much to overcome. Mac stayed with him, giving encouragement and watching the young Army man fade away. He cried as he rocked back and forth, holding Hamric in his arms. He was crying not just for Hamric, but also for all the others who had died.

Mac buried Hamric as best he could. There wasn't much dirt to throw over the body on a coral beach. Mac found a small depression, laid the body in it and covered it with coconut husks and leaves and other debris. He put a small marker on the grave and then waited until nightfall.

Across the International Dateline, it was December 17, 1944. On a snow-covered field near Malmedy, Belgium, during the Battle of the Bulge, German SS troops gunned down eighty American prisoners of war in what became known as the Malmedy Massacre. When word of the massacre reached the U.S. some weeks later, it made banner headlines across the country, and America was outraged. By the time word of the massacre at Palawan reached America, it received little attention—no headlines, no cries of indignation—as America listened and read about the huge American and Allied armies sweeping through Europe and the thousands of ships and men crossing the Pacific to Japan.

It was dark when Mac entered the water. He was the last prisoner to leave Palawan's Prison Camp 10A. Like Smitty, he would swim the channel alone. As he moved toward deeper water, he looked up into the night sky and saw the Southern Cross. He used it as his guiding light. He knew if he kept swimming toward it, he'd end up at Iwahig and hopefully get care and assistance from friendly Filipinos.

Meanwhile, Japanese troops on the island could breathe a little easier. The American invasion force had made only a feint toward Palawan. The Americans had bypassed the island and headed northeast toward Mindoro, the next island in the Philippine chain, where on December 15, the day after the Palawan Massacre, American troops had gone ashore.

When he entered the water and moved away from shore, Mac did not look back. Behind him were the bodies of his dead comrades, old friends whose burned, broken bodies were scattered about the prison. He'd miss Carl Mango, the camp doctor who had saved his life. Mac thought the doctor was a saint. And he would not forget the quiet little Air Force Sergeant Joseph Uballe of Boone, Iowa or Charlie (Pop) Sirfus, the Army Bandsman whose son, Johnny, had dated Glenn's sister. Had he lived, Pop would have been proud of his son. Johnny had joined the Marine Corps, and, just four months before the massacre, Private First Class Johnny Sirfus, under heavy enemy fire, had driven his amphibious vehicle, loaded with Marine infantrymen, ashore on the beach at Guam in the Marianas. For the next eight days, until the island was liberated, he had ferried in men, ammunition and food.

And not to be forgotten were the other Iowans, their bodies scattered about the prison compound: John Diaz of Osage, Glen Teel of Columbus Junction and Wilfred Kernes of Madrid. Mac also remembered Raymond (Rubber) Seagraves, who'd lost so much weight that his skin hung in folds. But then, they'd all lost weight, and a lot of it, during their stay on Palawan. And who could ever forget the tobacco-chewing John Warren, the camp barber who'd conned two Japanese guards into swallowing chewing tobacco, a mistake which would have sickened a horse.

It was an all-night swim. Mac would swim and then float a while. It was a gentler sea—no wind or high waves—and even as exhausted as he was, Mac was determined to swim the five miles. His legs and arms were numb and nearly lifeless, but he stayed with it. He did not think of anything—no thoughts of home, the massacre, or his dead friends—but keeping his eye on the Southern Cross and using what little energy he had left to keep going. Shortly before daybreak, his feet touched sand. He realized he'd missed his target, but not by much. He collapsed on the beach, unable to move, and he lay there for some time. A coconut washed up beside him. Mac grabbed it and tried to break it open. He was so weak, he had trouble cracking the shell. Finally, he managed to crack it on a rock and was able to drink the milk. Mac's hands and lips were so swollen from exposure to wind and saltwater that he couldn't eat the meat. He'd been without food and water for four days, and the once-husky Iowa Marine, who at one time had weighed 185 pounds, was now down to about 120 pounds. The weight loss wouldn't end there. He'd lose a few more pounds before he reached the southern tip of Palawan.

When Mac had regained some of his strength, he got up and started an awkward stumbling attempt at running. For all he knew, he was in enemy territory, and he wasn't about to be taken again. Mac barged through the jungle foliage where the leaves, like razors, cut into his bare thighs. When he could run no further, he sat down under a big tree, rested for a while and thought about all that had happened in the last few days. He knew he had to keep moving. He made it to water's edge and looked out at the bay. It looked like a short swim from where he was to Iwahig. He started swimming. He was about halfway across when again his strength gave out. He was about to go under for the final time when he saw a Filipino fish trap in the water. He moved as best he could to the trap and held on to one of the wooden poles which supported the net. Then he slowly pulled himself to the middle of the trap and passed out.

Free at Last

He slept through the night and was awakened shortly before dawn by the sounds of a village waking up. There were lights coming on in the huts, and he could smell the food which was being prepared for morning breakfast. He heard men talking on the beach and watched as they jumped into their barcos to check their fish traps. Mac didn't know whether he was in friendly territory, so he lay there quietly and watched the activity. Then, he saw them pointing his way. It appeared as if they were heading toward him, but their barcos swerved in the water, stopped and pulled another man out of the water. From what he could see, it appeared to be another American survivor. The Filipinos paddled to shore with the man and carried him into the village.

Mac was afraid to get their attention by yelling. He decided to wait and see if any Japanese trucks or troops came into the village. He waited and then tried to get up, just in case he had to make a run for it, but he was so tired he couldn't move. He lay there, numbed by fatigue—no trucks came, no screaming Japanese. For the first time in nearly two and a half years, he felt a wave of relief, for he was no longer a slave or even a hunted man. Freedom, home and family were getting a little closer.

A short while later the Filipinos returned to the shoreline, boarded their barcos and paddled out to check their fish traps. Mac was half submerged on the trap, but he raised up just enough to be spotted. The Filipinos moved quickly when they saw him. Paddling up to the trap, one of them said, "Hey Joe, you POW?" With a weak grin on his face, Mac said, "I was, but no longer." "Come with us! Come!" they said, but Mac was too weak to move. They moved in closer, lifted him off the trap and into the barco and paddled to shore. They didn't mention the other POW they'd found, and Mac didn't bring it up. For all he knew, they were friendly to the Japanese, and he was too frightened at that point to want to know the truth. When they reached shore, they carried him to a bamboo hut where they bathed him, cleaned all the sores he'd picked up during his escape and fed him what he still remembers today as the most wonderful fish and rice bread he had ever tasted. He waited for some word from them about the other prisoner they'd picked out of the water, but they said nothing.

He lay in the hut alone for some time. The tension, the fear of being hunted down and killed had left him, and lying there in that small hut was wonderful, but the quiet rest ended when a Filipino scout entered the hut and asked, "Do you know a Douglas W. Bogue?" Mac raised up off the cot and said, "I sure do!" "He's in the hut right next to yours," the scout said, "but he's hurt pretty bad." Mac asked if he could see him, so a couple of Filipinos helped him walk to the next hut. There was a joyous but low-key reunion. Both were too weak to do any more than talk. Bogue couldn't get up off the cot. His feet were so cut up from running along the coral beach that he couldn't walk. A doctor from Iwahig Penal Colony, Captain Bunie, came to the village and held Bogue down while Mac, as weak as he was, cut out the maggots which had imbedded in Bogue's feet. Then Bogue's feet were washed and bandaged. The two Marines talked some more. Bogue told Mac how he'd crawled under the barbed wire to make his escape, how he had met up with four other POWs who swam across the bay with him, how they had been separated during the night. He didn't know whether any of them had survived. Mac asked Bogue if Smitty was one of the men who made the swim. "No Mac, I'm sorry. I never saw him," said Bogue. "It was Martyn, Barta, Petry and Pacheco. I saw a bunch of other guys, too, Mac. But Smitty wasn't one of 'em."

They talked for a while longer, and then Mac returned to his hut to get some sleep. It was the first good night's sleep he'd had in three years, but still a fitful one. He woke up screaming several times during the night and then fell asleep again. It wouldn't be the last time he'd wake up screaming.

When he woke up the next morning, he was given more food and felt he was even being pampered by the villagers. It was wonderful. As he lay there on his cot, someone walked through the doorway of his hut. He didn't recognize the man at first, because he was silhouetted in the doorway of the darkened hut. But when the man moved closer, Mac recognized the turncoat Filipino scout, Pedro Pajie. Mac could hardly believe it. He couldn't help but smile and shake his head in disgust. He'd made it this far, and now the stupid son of a bitch in front of him was going to turn him over to the Japanese. He thought maybe they'd just kill him in the village. Bogue, too, for that matter. Mac threw up his arms and yelled at Pajie, "Well, when are the goddamn Japs coming after me, you rotten bastard?" Pedro Pajie just laughed and told Mac that he was not who Mac thought he was, but was spying on the Japanese and relaying all the information to U.S. forces. Pajie explained he had to play that role to get the Japanese to trust him, so he could count the number of planes and ammunition dumps the Japanese had on the island. He'd then take the information back to Iwahig and radio it to U.S. forces. Mac learned that not only was Pajie the Assistant Director of the Iwahig Penal Colony, he was in charge of all underground activities against the Japanese in that area.

According to Pajie, the Japanese had heard that American escapees were in the village and were headed to Iwahig to get them. The guerrilla leader had already radioed Australia informing them there were two more survivors of the Palawan Massacre. He gave Mac and Bogue some clothes and told them they would be leaving the village accompanied by three Filipino scouts who could not speak English. Pajie warned them not to talk or make any noise because they would be traveling near Japanese outposts.

Mac climbed on a water buffalo and Bogue rode a horse as the three scouts moved them along the path to freedom. They rode all night through the jungle. At times, they came within 300 yards of Japanese patrols. It was a slow and long journey south to Brookes Point.

They rode over the top of a hill on Christmas Eve, 1944, and looked down on the village of Inaguan just as the sun was setting. It was a beautiful sight. The scouts stopped for a moment, smiled and then, in almost perfect English, sang "God Bless America." Both Bogue and Mac had tears streaming down their faces when one of the scouts said, "My friends, you are now in the free Philippines!"

They continued their trek on Christmas Day, riding to the little village of Aborlan. A local guerrilla force would take over and escort them to Brookes Point. There was no activity in the village that day. It was a holiday for the Filipinos, and they stayed in their huts. Both Bogue and Mac could hear low-flying aircraft along the beach. They figured it was probably Japanese planes looking for the Palawan escapees. While Mac and Bogue stayed in their hut, Smitty was free at last. He climbed aboard a PBY bomber at Brookes Point, at the southern tip of Palawan, and flew out of Japanese territory to freedom.

That night, Mac heard chattering outside and went to investigate. Another Palawan survivor had been found. Fern Barta, one of those who had made the swim across the bay with Doug Bogue, came riding into the village with only a blanket covering his body. As they helped Barta off the horse, he saw Mac and moaned, "Oh, Mac, I'm hurt real bad!" Mac lifted the blanket and saw Barta's crotch. All he could see was blood and torn flesh. His scrotum had been ripped open, exposing his testicles. Mac took an even closer look and discovered that maggots were already at work on Barta's flesh.

Barta said he'd lost sight of the other swimmers but had finally made it to shore, where he started running through the jungle. He lost his bearings and climbed a coconut tree in an effort to determine where he was. The limb he was standing on broke, and Barta fell. The stub of the broken limb tore through his scrotum. It was an extremely painful wound, making it almost impossible to walk, but walk he did. Barta had been lost in the jungle for 10 days when he stumbled into the Iwahig Penal Colony. Filipino guerrillas escorted the wounded Barta to Inagauan and then to Aborlan, where he joined up with Mac and Doug Bogue.

Mac looked at the wound and then turned to the scouts who'd brought him into the camp. "My God, this man needs medical attention," he said. "He's got maggots crawling all over him!" The scouts helped Mac carry Barta into the hut. One of the guerrillas brought in some soap, tweezers and medicine. Mac soaked Barta's wound in the Filipino homemade medicine, a purple concoction—he would never discover just what it was—and then cleaned it with soap. Then Mac went to work on the maggots, counting them as he pulled them from Barta's crotch—52 of them in all. All Mac could do after that was to clean the dirt and grime from Barta's body and cover him with some dried brown leaves, another Filipino home remedy. It worked. Barta would live to father two children.

When Mac had finished with Barta, one of the scouts walked into the hut and told him that other men had survived the Palawan massacre. They had already been through the village and were probably home by now. Mac and Bogue had missed them by only a few days. "Names! Do you have any names of those guys?" they asked. One of the scouts read the names of the survivors off a piece of paper he carried: "Edwin Petry, William Balchus, Ernest Koblos, Eugene Nielsen, Albert Pacheco and Rufus Smith." Mac hung on the last name read. Heaving a sigh of relief, and with a big smile spreading across his face, he yelled, "My God, Smitty made it!"

The day after Christmas, 1944, the survivors pulled out of the village and, escorted by the Filipino scouts, headed south to Brookes Point at the southern tip of Palawan Island. After they arrived, each came down with a malarial attack. It took the three of them several days to come out of it, but there was plenty of time. It would be a long wait, and it would give them time to gain some weight and regain some of the vigor drained from them by the hard years spent as slave laborers. Mac was down to 118 pounds when he arrived at Brookes Point, having lost an additional two pounds to the malarial attacks. Now he was getting good food every day. Much of it was served to him by a seven-year-old Filipino girl, Mary Anne Major, the daughter of Captain Maziro Major, leader of the guerrilla movement for all of southern Palawan Island. Mac had first met Mary Ann when the little girl appeared in the doorway of his hut. She stared at the young American for a few moments, and then said, "You want a drink?" Mac laughed and said, "Yes." The water was the best medicine he could get at this point. He needed all the liquids he could get. The little girl brought him the water and then placed her arm next to his. She was fascinated by the difference in skin color. As little as she was, Mary Anne would never forget the Americans, and they would never forget her, as she tended to them every day. In later years, she came to the United States to live and went looking for them.

Mac didn't want to spend the rest of the war waiting for rescue. He had a plan. He told the Filipino guerrilla chief at Brookes Point that he planned to make his way by boat to the small island of Balabac, which was located about 19 miles southwest of the southern tip of Palawan. From there, he planned to sail to Borneo, a much larger island located about 38 miles north of Balabac Island. Then he would make his way to Australia. That was Mac's plan, but when U.S. headquarters in Australia heard about it from the guerrilla chief, they sent a radio message to Brookes Point which said, "Tell those men to stay where they are!"

Mac was taking it easy in his hut one morning, thinking about home and family and when he'd be able to see them again. Mac jumped from his cot when he heard a couple of the villagers yell, "Submarine! Submarine!" He ran as fast as he could to the beach, but by the time he got there, the sub had already submerged. It had floated a raft containing wooden crates ashore. The crates contained metal canisters of .30-caliber shells for the M1 carbines the guerrillas used to fight the Japanese. By this time, Mac felt strong enough, and he volunteered to help carry the crates into the village. When he set it on the ground and glanced down at the stenciled lettering on the crate, he choked up. It was almost better than a letter from home. Stamped on the crate was "Des Moines, Iowa Ordnance Plant." The plant was only eight miles from his home in Urbandale, and he would discover later that his mother, Dessa, had been working at the plant since the beginning of the war.

12

Freedom

Final rescue came January 21, when the guerrillas received a radio message saying there would be a PBY flying to the Point to pick up the three survivors. It was an anxious day for the three men as they waited for the plane which would take them into friendly territory away from Palawan. About nine that morning, they heard the big PBY and the fighters that accompanied it. The scouts climbed to the top of the coconut trees and lighted smudge pots, which signaled an all-clear for the plane to land. The big Navy bomber sent up a white spray as its hull skimmed over the waves, then it slowly settled in the water while a half-dozen fighter planes circled overhead providing cover. When the PBY pulled in close to shore and opened its side hatch, Mac, Bogue and Barta climbed aboard. They were met by two smiling sailors who handed each of them a bottle of pop and a candy bar, their first "sweets" in well over three years. They swigged the pop and gobbled down the candy bars as the big plane gained speed and bounced off the water heading to Mindanao, where they refueled. From there, it was on to a U.S. base at Tacloban on the Island of Leyte, where the three boarded a hospital ship, the USS Tangier, and waited.

January 19, 1944, was a sunny, windy day in Urbandale. It had been warmer than usual in the first half of January, and the temperature would climb to 42 degrees today. There was no snow to contend with. Mac's mother, Dessa, hearing a knock at the front door, opened it to find a Western Union messenger. She was handed a telegram, something thousands of American mothers had received and opened reluctantly, fearing the worst. Dessa was no different, but when she started reading, it would be another memorable day. It was good news, great news, about her Marine Corps son, Glenn McDole. The telegram read:

My dear Mr. And Mrs. McDole: I have the pleasure of informing you that according to confidential information just received in this headquarters, your son, Private First Class Glenn W. McDole, U.S. Marine Corps, has escaped from the Japanese prison camp in which he was interned. He is in friendly hands, but may be unable to communicate with his family.

The telegram advised the McDoles not to tell anyone, for fear Mac might be captured again by the Japanese, but by that time Mac was in a safe harbor on board the hospital ship in Leyte.

Dessa McDole didn't waste time. She called the Urbandale school and asked that daughter, Dolores, and son, Joe, be sent home. Then she called Colleen and Max where they worked and told them to come home The school's principal, William Roseman, fearing bad news, escorted little Joe home. Dessa told Roseman what had happened and told him not to tell anyone. He kept the McDole family secret until the day they received a letter from Mac saying he'd returned to the "Good ol' U.S. of A" and would be home soon.

Leyte, Philippine Islands

Mac, Bogue and Barta had bunks below deck on the Navy hospital ship. When they boarded, sailors on deck looked at the three scrawny men as if they were shell-shocked loonies. They knew nothing about the three patients or what they had endured for the past three years. Mac, Bogue and Barta went below deck to their quarters and waited for three days. A Navy officer came below and told them Admiral Barby wanted to talk to them.

When the three survivors walked into the Admiral's quarters, he took one look at them and said, "My God, you fellas look bad." Mac had not gained any weight during his two weeks at Brookes Point; the malarial attacks had seen to that. Until the attacks, he had weighed about 113 pounds. Now that he was eating a lot of Navy Chow, as much as he wanted, he was gaining weight. The Admiral said, "You guys look like you've been through hell, and I want to know what happened." He gave each man a can of beer, then told them to sit down, relax and tell him what they'd been through. They told their story. They left nothing out. When they had finished, over an hour later, the Admiral said, "My God, you guys have been through hell. First thing in the morning you're going to be on your way to Washington, D.C."

They had priority the next day in getting a flight back to the U.S. They were bumping people off flights so they could head home and tell their story to the War Crimes Branch in Washington. Before they left Leyte, they were ordered to tell no one who they were or what they had been through. The Navy felt their story might leak out and endanger the lives of other prisoners who might still be on the island.

They took off across the Pacific for home. The first leg of the trip, to Hawaii, was pleasant enough, but while the plane was being refueled, a new passenger boarded the plane and sat next to them as they lifted off for the California coast. He was an Army Major, and he struck up a conversation with them. He questioned them. In fact, he never stopped talking, which made the final leg of the trip home less than pleasant. It was almost a one-way conversation. The man said, "I heard there are a couple of escaped POWs on board." Doug Bogue said, "Yeh, we heard the same thing." The guy didn't let up. "I wonder where they are?" he asked. Mac shrugged and told him, "I suppose they're probably some of the guys in back on the stretchers."

The officer rambled on incessantly across the Pacific, always questioning, but he had no success. When the final touchdown came many hours later in San Diego, the inquisitor confessed he'd been sent on the trip to make sure they could be trusted to keep their mouths shut. He said since he felt they could be trusted for the remainder of the trip, he wouldn't accompany them the rest of the way to Washington. He told them he was happy they'd stonewalled him, because then he'd be able to stay in San Diego and visit with his family.

It was a bright and sunny, typical southern California day when Mac stepped off the plane. As his feet touched the pavement, he knelt and kissed the ground and vowed never to leave the U.S. again. "Free at last!" he thought. Little did he know he would make one final trip overseas at war's end.

Mac, Bogue and Barta weren't in San Diego long. They boarded another Navy plane and headed toward Washington, landing in Omaha for refueling and then on to Chicago, where bad weather grounded them. They finished the trip to Washington by train and then spent about a week telling their story and answering questions. All of it was put on paper for future use at the war crimes trials in Japan.

When Mac first arrived in Washington, an officer kept asking Mac if he knew of any other Marines from Urbandale. He'd say, "No," and then the officer would say, "Are you sure?" When they walked into an office for interrogation, Glenn was met by a fellow Urbandale Marine, Ida McDivitt, a member of what was then called the Marine Corps Women's Reserve. She was stationed at Headquarters Marine Corps in Washington. They had known one another in school, and Ida lived just four blocks from Mac's home in Urbandale.

Glenn McDole meets a hometown girl, Ida McDivitt, at Marine Corps Headquarters in Washington, D.C. (U.S. War Department).

When the Navy and Marines had finished with them, it was time to
go home—Bogue to California, Barta to Oregon and Glenn McDole to
Iowa. Glenn was told that what he went through on Palawan Island was
to be kept secret, and he'd be notified as to when he could talk about it.
They boarded the train at Washington's Union Station and headed west
for their first leave and the first meeting with their families and loved ones
in over three years. By now, all three had put on some weight and were

getting back in shape. Since their arrival at the hospital ship in Leyte, they never left anything on their plates, and the eating binge continued.

It was Glenn McDole's 24th birthday, February 6, 1945, when the train pulled into the station in Ames. He'd planned on surprising his family by walking into their home in Urbandale, but word had leaked out that he was headed home. As the train pulled into the station, Barta yelled, "Mac, by the way you've described your family, I swear to God that's them looking in the window right now!"

Mac glanced through the window, and a big grin spread across his face—"I'll be go to hell, that's Margaret and Colleen!" He got up from his seat and shot toward the exit. Just as he bounded from the last step of the train he spotted them—all of them but one, his father, David. Mom, Max, little Joe, Colleen, Margaret and LeRoy Sexton, his old boxing buddy from his high school days. What a greeting it was, a time for hugs, kisses and tears. The man who had left Urbandale as a nineteen-year-old Marine in

This photograph was taken during the Depression of the '30s at the McDole farmstead in Nebraska. Glenn's dad is on the left with his arms around two of Glenn's sisters. Young teenager Glenn McDole is on the right, and his mother, Dessa, is in front of him. The elder Mac McDole died a year to the day before the Palawan Massacre.

November of 1940 shed tears, too. LeRoy Sexton was no longer just a box-ing buddy, but was his brother-in-law. He'd married Glenn's sister, Colleen.

On the car ride back to Urbandale, they told him about his father, the man who'd spent so much time with him hunting and fishing when he was a boy. The elder McDole had died December 14, 1943, exactly one year before the massacre and the day Mac buried himself in the garbage pile on Palawan Island.

The War Crimes Trials

On November 25, 1945, nearly two months after the formal Japanese surrender aboard the Battleship Missouri, Glenn McDole was released from active duty in the Marine Corps. He signed on as an Active Reservist in the Corps. He was back to wearing civilian clothes and wore the Marine Green only at reserve meetings. He settled down in Urbandale and started taking classes at the American Institute of Business. Life was returning to normal, and some of the scars inflicted upon him during the war were beginning to fade. But the memory of what had happened to him and the other prisoners on Palawan would never go away, and not a day went by that he didn't recall some event, some obscenity, that occurred at Puerto Princesa's prison camp. He got in touch with one of his prison camp bud-dies on Palawan, Walt Ditto, who lived in Des Moines. It was Ditto and Robert May who were so badly beaten for planning an escape that they had to be taken off the island and returned to Manila. May had also sur-vived the war.

Mac and Ditto became buddies and spent time together when they weren't working or attending classes. Mac was taking courses at the insti-tute when, on a warm summer evening, they headed downtown for a beer or two. They were standing on the corner talking when a little boy ran up to them. Looking at Ditto, he said, "Walt, we missed our street car! Can you give us a ride home?" Walt said, "Sure, Johnny, who's with you?" "Just my sister," he answered. "Go get her," Walt said, "and we'll give you a ride home."

When little Johnny's sister walked up, Cupid's arrow hit Mac dead center. He was awestruck, nearly rolled back on his heels by the 18-year-old woman who stood in front of him. He had never seen anyone so beau-tiful. They started dating. On August 10, 1946, Glenn McDole married Betty Moody, Walt Ditto's next door neighbor. Betty's brother, Bill, was best man at a simple ceremony in Adel, Iowa.

On August 13, 1947, another of Mac's dreams came true. He was accepted by the Iowa Highway Patrol. After training, his first duty station was at Creston. But the duties of a highway patrolman would have to wait a while. He had received a letter from the War Crimes Branch in Washington, asking if he'd be available to testify at the war crimes trials to be held in Japan. Mac didn't hesitate. He asked for and received a leave of absence from the patrol, and shortly after that he was on his way to Japan. Yokosuka was his first stop and he met one of the other Palawan survivors, Sergeant Doug Bogue, who had remained in the service and was stationed in Japan. The two helped identify the former guards and officers at Palawan. In all, 33 men had been found and were held for trial. There would have been more, but many of them had been left behind to die on Palawan—killed in action when American forces finally landed or lost in the rain forests and mountains on the big island. It was an anxious and angry time for both Mac and Doug Bogue. Well before U.S. occupation forces moved into Japan, thousands of records, dispatches, orders and other reports had been burned by the Japanese military. This allowed still more soldiers accused of war crimes to meld into Japanese society with new names and occupations. Nevertheless, some of the Palawan prison guards and officers had been located.

Mac was sent to Tokyo to identify those who had been arrested and jailed in Tokyo's Sugamo Prison. Again, he told his story of the Palawan Massacre. This was not a pleasant experience for him. Seeing the former guards made him nervous and distraught. His hatred for the Japanese had only increased since the end of the war. When he walked into the room where interrogations were to take place, he realized he'd have to work hard at controlling his emotions. It was very difficult for him to maintain his composure while looking at the men he'd dreamed about killing while he was a prisoner on Palawan.

The prisoner interrogations took place in Tokyo's Dai-Ichi Building. A tall building spared from the devastating fire bombings of B29s during the latter stages of the war, it would be General MacArthur's headquarters while he reshaped postwar Japanese society. The prisoners were brought into the interrogation room one at a time. As they stepped off the elevator, they were told to face left and then front so Glenn and Doug Bogue could identify them.

The first prisoner off the elevator was the camp's chief cook, Manichi Nishitoni. Mac nearly lost control when Nishitoni entered the room. No one heard Mac mumble, "You no good rotten bastard!" Mac's hands were trembling. He was sweating, and his rage was making him sick. But he took a couple of deep breaths, recovered his composure, and helped question the prisoner. Nishitoni denied everything. When they started to take Nishatoni back to his prison cell, Sergeant Doug Bogue moved quickly. To the surprise of the military police and officers in the room, he landed a solid blow to Nishatoni's head. When they pulled Bogue away, one officer asked him why he had struck the prisoner. Bogue replied, "For the same reason you're going to hang him!"

One of the next prisoners to face his accusers was Master Sergeant Taichi Deguchi, the brute who had enjoyed beating prisoners on a daily basis and who stood accused of murder and beatings. When Deguchi stepped off the elevator, he stared straight ahead, his face expressionless. This was the man Mac wanted to kill, but this time he controlled his emotions. In the interrogation room, the former Acting Commanding Officer of the Kempei Tai Unit (Military Police) of the Palawan prisoner of war camp denied everything with the simple unemotional reply of, "No!"

One prison guard after another was questioned, but not one of them would admit guilt. When Kuta Schugota, better known as Smiley to the POWs, was told to turn and face the window, he spotted Mac on the other side of the glass. He bowed his head, and, when brought through the door, he fell to his knees and crawled across the floor to the table where Mac sat. He put his hands on the table and sobbed, "Oh, Macky Dole, I thought

Marine Master Sergeant Doug Bogue points out the location of the trench bomb shelters at the war crimes trial in Yokohama, Japan (U.S. War Department).

you had been killed." Mac assured him that he hadn't. He told Smiley he'd come to Japan to see that justice was done. Then he asked for Smiley's help. They started asking Smiley questions, the same questions they'd posed to the other guards, but Smiley wouldn't cooperate and denied all of it. He would not confirm what the other guards had done. Mac went into one of his rages. He yelled, "Ya know, Smiley, you were always kind to us. You'd let us eat bananas and coconuts, and you were the only guard who treated us with kindness. I never saw you raise your hand to hit one of us, but if you don't tell us what you know, I'll tell them you were the meanest son of a bitch there was! Understand?" Shaken and still in denial, Smiley was taken back to Sugamo Prison.

When there were breaks in the courtroom action, Mac had time to walk the streets of Tokyo, then teeming with thousands of people. Several times during his walks around Tokyo, he saw the man he considered to be one of his Corregidor comrades, General Douglas MacArthur. Mac stood in awe as MacArthur's motorcade drove toward his headquarters in the Dai-Ichi Building. Everyone on the street, vendors, shoppers, and those on their way to work, bowed as MacArthur passed. The man who was responsible for turning Japan from war and conquest to peace and prosperity was truly, as historian William Manchester concluded in his book, an "American Caesar." Mac wondered if the general remembered him and their private little talk about home and family one evening, just outside his command post on bomb-pocked Corregidor, or the General's casual strolls to the bomb shelter when Japanese bombers appeared over the island.

The questioning continued for weeks before the trial, and Mac stayed on, hoping to see a just conclusion to what had happened to him and his fellow prisoners. He was having lunch in the Dai-Ichi Building's cafeteria when an MP came to his table and told him that a prisoner in Sugamo Prison, a guy named Schugota wanted to see him. At first, he couldn't figure out who he might be, then it dawned on him that it was Smiley. He went to the prison that afternoon. When he walked into Smiley's cell, he hardly recognized the former guard. Smiley looked haggard and sick. He had not been eating. "All right, Smiley, what do you want? I don't want anymore lies from you, and I want the truth!" Smiley looked at Mac and said he'd tell all he knew. Mac yelled to the guards. They escorted Smiley back to the Dai-Ichi building, where Smiley told prosecutors everything they wanted to know—the orders they'd received from Manila, information he'd picked up about the massacre, and the beatings and torture he'd witnessed but had never taken part in. He named names and filled in the dates. When it was over, they whisked Smiley back to Sugamo Prison.

The interrogations of the former prison guards and officers, and the depositions of the former Palawan prisoners took several weeks. When it was over, it was time for Glenn McDole to head home to Iowa and get back to living a normal life. He'd done everything they'd asked, and there was no need for him to stay for the trials in Yokohama and Tokyo. But shortly before his departure, he thought again of the smiling little Japanese guard, the only one on Palawan Island to show any kindness to the prisoners. He was still in Sugamo Prison. Mac knew Smiley wasn't guilty of any crime, and felt he had to do something for him. Mac talked to the military prosecutors, and they agreed: Smiley would be released from prison. Mac asked that he be allowed to go to the prison and be the first to tell Smiley that he was a free man.

When Mac saw Smiley enter the room at Sugamo Prison, the former prison guard looked worse than he had the last time they'd met. The two men stood there looking at one another for a moment. Finally, Mac asked, "Smiley, how would you like to go home?" "Oh please don't joke, Macky Dole!" Smiley pleaded. Mac smiled and said, "This is no joke, Smiley. You helped us prosecute those guilty of war crimes, and, in all fairness, you've never done anything to harm any of us. You're free to go home to your family." Smiley was humbled and overjoyed by what he'd just heard, and he asked to shake hands. When Mac held out his hand, Smiley grabbed it and held it to his bosom and cried like a baby. He told Mac he was married, had two daughters, and painted signs for a living. "When I go home I tell my daughters, Macky Dole, an American Prisoner of War saved my life. Thank you so much!" The former Palawan guard stepped back and saluted Mac and then turned and walked out the door, a free man in a country which was about to experience a huge cultural change.

After the meeting with Smiley, Mac packed up, said goodbye to Doug Bogue and others he'd been working with and headed back to Iowa. When his plane lifted off the runway in Tokyo, he thought about the 33 Japanese officers and men who would go to trial. He was sure they would all be convicted and was almost certain all of them would face the gallows. It didn't turn out that way. There was a concerted effort, a mad rush following the war, to return Japan to normalcy by instituting a democratic government, even giving Japanese women the right to vote. There was too much at stake in the Pacific. The overall effort by General MacArthur, considered godlike by the Japanese, was to ward off Soviet expansion in the far east.

Many weeks after Mac's return to the U.S, the trials ended and the verdicts were returned. For the survivors and the dead of the Palawan Massacre, the scales of justice were decidedly well off-balance. Of the thirty-three Japanese officers and men brought up on war crimes charges in connection with the Palawan Massacre, only sixteen men were put on trial, and six of them were acquitted.

At his trial in Tokyo, Lieutenant General Seiichi Terada, Commanding General of the 2nd Air Division on Negros Island, never denied sending the order to execute the prisoners of Palawan Barracks. His argument
was that he had received no written orders which placed him in control
of the battalion on Palawan. As far as Terada was concerned, command of
the battalion was still in the hands of the 4th Air Division headquartered
in Manila. He had been told he was to take command, but there had been
no written order. Terada wanted a written order. He knew nothing about
the airfield battalion at Puerto Princesa, he said, and unless he had a written order, he felt it was not his responsibility. That was his defense.

When General Terada had received the message from Captain Kojima,
commanding officer of the 131st Airfield Battalion, asking what should be
done with the prisoners if American forces landed, Terada messaged General Tominaga in Manila asking for instructions concerning the fate of the
prisoners. Tominaga, according to Terada, said it would be best to elimi-
nate the prisoners. Terada felt he had to relay an order of execution; after
all, he thought, this was a smaller unit requesting advice, and he felt oblig-
ated to provide it. The message was sent, and the American POWs were
slaughtered.

When the war ended, General Terada was arrested and held in Tokyo's
Sugamo Prison. When the military commission trying war crimes was
formed, he was charged with violating the Laws and Customs of War during a time of war between the United States of America, its allies, its depen-
dencies, and Japan. There were 13 specifications in the charge against
Terada, among them: denying prisoners the status of prisoners of war;
compelling prisoners to work on construction and maintenance projects
having a direct relationship to war operations against American and Allied
forces; exposing the prisoners to the dangers of a combat zone; and compelling prisoners to stand on the runways during American bombing raids.
Terada was held directly responsible for the December 14, 1944, massacre.
He was found guilty on all but four of the specifics, and, on November 8,
1948, General Terada was sentenced to a life term in Tokyo's Sugamo
Prison.

Master Sergeant Taichi Deguchi, probably the most feared man at
Palawan Barracks, was also charged with violating the Laws and Customs
of War. There were six charges against him: that he beat and then killed
two POWs, Seldon White and Earl Vance Wilson; that he beat and abused
seven American POWs; that he beat, abused, and threw Walter Ditto and
Robert Carl May into the Palawan Barracks dungeon and held them there
for three months without adequate clothing, food, water and sanitary facilities; and that he mistreated, abused and killed two unidentified American POWs when he ordered his men to beat them to death. There was one

additional charge, that on or about December 14, 1944, he took part in the slaughter of 139 American POWs at Palawan Barracks Camp 10A.

Deguchi pleaded not guilty to all charges, but the evidence was overwhelming. On November 8, 1948, before a military commission in Yokohama, Deguchi was sentenced to be hanged by the neck until dead. The commission ruled that the sentence would not be carried out until confirmed by the Supreme Commander for the Allied Powers, General Douglas MacArthur.

Superior Private Tomisaburo Sawa had landed with his unit at Puerto Princesa in August, 1944. He helped maintain the airfield and guarded the surrounding area. When the original guard unit at Palawan Barracks pulled out, Sawa, a member of the 131st Airfield Battalion, helped guard the 150 Americans remaining at the prison camp.

While being held for trial at Tokyo's Sugamo Prison, Sawa opened a blank loose-leaf notebook and began writing a letter of confession. He admitted his part in the brutal beatings, bayonetings, beheadings, shootings and burnings prior to and during that fateful day of Deccember 14, 1944. He told it all, including his own brutal treatment of prisoners working at the airfield. He admitted that he preferred cutting the thin-skinned prisoners after he had knocked them to the ground. He told of his involvement the day of the massacre, how he shot and killed three POWs as he stood on the veranda of the prison barracks, how POWs, many of them on fire, ran from their bomb shelters begging to be shot.

For his part in the Palawan massacre, Sawa received a five-year prison term, but it was reduced to three and a half years for time already served.

Manichi Nishitani, the maniacal head cook at Palawan Barracks, was sentenced on a separate docket to five years in prison for the beatings he'd committed.

Lieutenant General Kizo Mikama, Commanding General of the 4th Air Division, 4th Air Army, received a twelve-year prison sentence for his part in the massacre.

Lieutenant Colonel Mamoru Fushimi, who headed up the 11th Air Sector Unit of the 4th Air Army, would spend ten years in prison. Four others were sentenced to terms ranging from two to five years. Six of those charged in the Palawan Massacre were acquitted.

Shortly after Deguchi's death sentence was pronounced, General Douglas MacArthur signed an order commuting the Sergeant Major's sentence to 30 years in prison. Neither Deguchi nor Lieutenant General Terada would serve the long sentences handed down to them. A general amnesty for all Japanese war crimes prisoners was announced in 1958, and both men walked out of Tokyo's Sugamo Prison.

Lieutenant General Masaharu Homma, Commanding General of the

All that remained of the Palawan thatched roof cooking shed, with its two barrels used to boil rice for the camp's 300 prisoners (U.S. War Department).

Japanese 14th Army which invaded the Philippines in December 1941, after the attack on Pearl Harbor, was not so lucky. Following the Japanese surrender in 1945, he returned to Tokyo, where he was charged with having been responsible for the Bataan Death March and for condoning other atrocities. Found guilty by a military tribunal, Homma was returned to the Philippines, to the city of Los Baños, where on April 3, 1946, he was executed by a military firing squad.

Lieutenant General Tomoyuki Yamashita, the Tiger of Malaya, had been sent to command the defense of the Philippines against American and Allied forces. Badly beaten in both the Leyte and Luzon campaigns, he held out until after the general surrender was announced from Tokyo. Yamashita was tried for war crimes committed by the Japanese Army across the Thai and Malay peninsulas in 1941 and 1942, and in the Philippines in 1944. He was tried and convicted, although he denied knowing anything about those crimes. After the death sentence was announced, he was taken to Manila, where, on February 23, 1946, he was hanged.

For some unexplained reason, the Philippine government charged

General Aeiichi Terada, second from left, at his war crimes trial in Yokohama, Japan (U.S. War Department).

guerrilla leader Pedro Pajie with treason when the war ended. When he went on trial, depositions from both Glenn McDole and Rufus Smith helped clear Pajie of the charges.

There have been great changes in the Philippines since the dark days of World War II, but the Filipino people have not forgotten what happened there. Scattered around the country, there are reminders of the Pacific War.

13

Back Home

Mac settled down and began work as a highway patrolman. He liked the work and earned the respect of the officers above him and those that patrolled the roads with him. When time permitted, he fished Iowa's lakes in the summer and hunted pheasant, ducks and geese in the fall and winter months.

There was one break in his twenty-nine-year career with the highway patrol. He was called into active duty again in 1950 during the Korean War. He saw no combat during that conflict, but was stationed for about a year at Camp Pendleton, California, handling classified reports coming in from Korea. He wasn't alone this time. His wife, Betty, was with him. The Marine Corps sent Mac home to civilian life in late 1951, and he hung up the uniform for good.

As a highway patrolman, Mac was stationed at several posts in Iowa, including Creston, Mount Ayr, Osceola and Des Moines. He was a sergeant stationed in Des Moines when, in December of 1960, he was called into Colonel Dave Herrick's office. Just before that, fellow officers at the patrol's state headquarters had told him he was in a lot of trouble with the chief and that he'd have some explaining to do. They asked him what he had done to get Herrick so angry. Mac was befuddled and very anxious. He couldn't figure out what he'd done to incur the wrath of the patrol's highest ranking officer. He waited anxiously outside the chief's office for the word to go in. As anxious as he was, he dreaded walking into the chief's office. The call came. The Colonel had a stern look on his face and was shuffling papers when Mac entered the office. Mac feared the worst. Herrick took his time moving papers around, apparently Mac's personnel file, and said, "You know, Mac, we've never had a patrol office at Storm Lake.

How would you like to be in charge up there?" Mac couldn't believe what he'd just heard. And what came next was even more astonishing: He'd been promoted to lieutenant. He'd been a sergeant for only six months. He had applied for the higher rank when the opening was announced, but he never thought he'd get it. The McDole family would spend the rest of Mac's career with the patrol at Storm Lake. Along the way, he had two children, Glenda and Kathy.

He wasn't the only one wearing a uniform in the McDole household. Mac's wife, Betty, was a Storm Lake police matron and meter maid. While he kept an eye on the state's highways, Betty patrolled the city's business section, ticketing overtime parkers.

Mac retired from the Iowa Highway Patrol in 1976, but he wasn't through with life in law enforcement. He joined the Polk County Sheriff's Department as Chief of Patrol, where he served for 12 years and retired in 1989. His daughter, Kathy, has followed in her father's footsteps and is a patrol officer in the Sheriff's department. His other daughter, Glenda, is administrative secretary to the dean of Des Moines Area Community College in Ankeny.

Good friend and former Palawan prisoner, Walt Ditto, who introduced Glenn to his wife, Betty, joined the highway patrol after the war and later went into the insurance business. He was killed in an auto accident in Des Moines.

Remember the little seven-year-old Filipino girl, daughter of the guerrilla leader, Captain Maziro Major? She was the one who fed and cared for the prisoners at Brookes Point while they rested and waited for their flight to freedom. Mary Ann grew up and married a doctor, Valentino Ancheta, and moved to America. The doctor and Mary Ann settled in Algoma, Wisconsin. While reading her hometown newspaper one day, she spotted an announcement by six American survivors of Palawan who were looking for their rescuers. Mary Ann grabbed the phone and called Glenn McDole. Forty-four years after the massacre, in 1989, there was a tearful and happy reunion at Mary Ann's home in Algoma. Mary Ann's brother, Robert, who also played a role in the rescue, still lives on Palawan. Their father, Maziro Major, retired to Manila. Glenn and Mary Ann still keep in touch.

Glenn has also kept in touch with the Palawan prison camp's shoemaker, Don Thomas. When Thomas returned to Iowa after the war, he went to college on the GI Bill. He and his wife, Jean, live in Winterset, Iowa, where he taught high school art classes for thirty-three years. Don and Jean celebrated their 50th wedding anniversary in 1997.

Glenn McDole has received many honors over the years. In 1975 a large group of friends and neighbors gathered for Storm Lake's Memorial Day Parade of Flags to honor the former Marine, who was then a mid-

One of several reunions Glenn McDole has had with the Filipino girl who fed and cared for him after his flight to freedom. Mary Ann Ancheta, second from left, married Dr. Valentino Ancheta, far left. They live in Algoma, Wisconsin. Next to Mary Ann is her father, former Captain Mazior Major; Glenn; his wife, Betty; and Mary Ann's brother, Robert, who still lives on Palawan. In the rear are Glenn's daughters, Kathy, left, and Glenda, right, with Kathy's friend, Heather Sanderson, center.

dle-aged Highway Patrol lieutenant. It was to be his day. Two hundred forty flags fluttered in the breeze as they named that Flag Day in honor of a man who served his country so courageously and then came home to serve his state as a law officer.

He fought off tears as they played the National Anthem, and while the music was playing, he said a silent prayer for those, his buddies, who didn't make it home.

In a ceremony at the Iowa Statehouse in 1985, Glenn received still another honor, won during the war but not awarded at that time. Governor Terry Brandstad pinned the Bronze Medal/Combat V on McDole. Mac deserved that medal. He fought to the end at Ft. Hughes on Corregidor, did his part in sustaining the lives of his friends at Palawan, and survived a bloody massacre. His flight to freedom, and his participation in telling the story of what had happened at Palawan alerted U.S. forces in the Philippines and the Pacific to move quickly to the prison camps to save the lives of other POWs during the final days of World War II.

Top: Two former Palawan POWs, Glenn McDole, left, and Eugene Nielsen, place a wreath at the burial site of the POWs killed on Palawan Island. *Bottom:* Glenn McDole bows his head as he prays and remembers his comrades left behind on Palawan Island (Kathy and Glenda McDole).

Governor Terry Brandstad (light suit, back to camera) pins the Bronze Medal/ Silver V on Glenn McDole in a 1985 ceremony at the Iowa Statehouse.

October 4, 2003, was a sunny, warm day at Jefferson Barracks National Cemetery in St. Louis. About a hundred people, friends and relatives of those killed in the massacre at Palwan's Camp 10A, gathered to dedicate a new grave marker for 123 of the 139 victims buried there in a single grave.

Two survivors of the massacre, Glenn McDole and Eugene Nielsen, were on hand for the ceremony. The two men told what happened to them on the day of the massacre, and then the two World War II veterans placed a wreath at the site and dedicated a new plaque, which gave more details of what happened on that terrible day, December 14, 1944.

Now in his 80s, Mac and his wife, Betty, have had some major health problems, but both have managed to overcome them, and they lead an active life. So far, he hasn't hired out the job of mowing his yard, and he's kept active with church work, the American Legion, the Veterans of Foreign Wars and the Shrine. He's still talking to schools, churches, civic groups and veterans organizations about Palawan. Once a year, he travels to whatever city the 4th Marine Regiment of World War II (The China Marines) has chosen to hold its annual reunion, and it's a good bet he'll attend more of those meetings in the years ahead. In all his years as a

Glenn McDole tells a crowd of over 100 relatives and friends of those who died on Palawan what happened on December 14, 1944 (Kathy and Glenda McDole)

member of the Iowa Highway Patrol and as Chief of Patrol for the Polk County Sheriff's Office, he has never stopped being a U.S. Marine, always referring to himself as a "former U.S. Marine." Although it's difficult for those who haven't worn Marine green to understand, there are no ex-Marines.

Glenn McDole's love for his country and his comrades in arms— those still alive and those that never made it home—has never faltered. At his home on Sharmin Drive in Ankeny, Iowa, the American flag is flown 24 hours a day, and Glenn adheres to flag etiquette. At dusk, a sensor turns on a spotlight which illuminates Old Glory during the nighttime hours. He always takes part in ceremonies on those days throughout the year when America honors its war dead.

Semper Fidelis

14

The Men

Glenn McDole never returned to the Philippines or Japan after he returned from the war crimes trials. He never left the U.S. except for fishing trips into Canada. Although he has thought about returning to Palawan, he hasn't made a concerted effort to do so. He would like to see the beach again where he hid following his escape and visit the site of what was once Palawan Barracks Camp 10A. He wonders if the Japanese ever discovered the shallow grave where he buried Dane Hamric under a layer of coconut husks and palm leaves. The wave action of the Sulu Sea has long since washed away all the blood, all traces of what happened on that beach so many years ago, but it has not been erased from the minds of the survivors, many of whom have agonized over it all their adult lives.

Glenn McDole does not believe in ghosts, but his buddies—alive and dead—are with him every day. He has fought off his anguish by talking about it. He has told the story of the massacre and the terrible Pacific War to church, school, business and veteran's organizations. At over 80 years of age, he's still making speaking engagements, at least 15 a year. Many of those are return engagements. No one would disagree with Glenn McDole that, mentally, he's whipped the nightmare of Palawan. However, his wife, Betty, will tell you that there are still nights when he comes out of a fitful sleep and paces the floor for awhile before he can go back to bed.

We'd like to believe, and so would Glenn, that Rufus Smith, or Smitty, had the same good mental health as Mac. Smitty went home to Hughes Springs, Texas, after the war, married a southern belle named Bess, and had four children: Glenn, Don, Nita and Kathy. He was a steel worker in his hometown. He died April 14, 1994.

Roy Henderson, who was taken off Palawan Island after suffering severe head injuries sustained in a fight with another prisoner, spent the rest of the war in Manila's Bilibid Prison. When the war ended, he went back home to Hooks, Texas, married a girl named Margaret, and had four children, Shelia, Etta, Dana and Glenna. He retired from the Army Ammunition Depot and died in May of 1978, the same day the memorial and burial plot for the Palawan victims was dedicated at Jefferson Barracks Military Cemetery in St. Louis.

Survivor William Balchus of Shenandoah, Pennsylvania, is 80 years old. Balchus is in failing health and "takes life from day to day." He won't talk about Palawan and said he's really trying to forget. He tries every day to forget it, but he admits it's still with him.

Survivor Elmo Deal of North Highlands, California, is in good spirits and good health. He was in the Coast Artillery at Topside on Corregidor when captured and showed no signs of distress when we talked to him. He's a jolly, 80-year-old former jeweler who retired at age 65.

Douglas Bogue retired with the rank of Major in the Marine Corps and lived in Lompoc, California, with his wife. Bogue would not talk about the massacre with anyone, and that includes his wife, Betty, and their three daughters. He would get very angry when asked about his life in the prison camp and his escape—not one word about Palawan could be gotten from him. Doug Bogue passed away in March 2004.

When Thomas (Pop) Daniels went home to Texas after the war, he lived the life of a hermit. He wasn't above shooting at someone trying to come onto his property. They found him sitting in a chair, dead from a heart attack, with a rifle on his lap. It was Daniels who squatted, paralyzed with fear, at the escape hole in the bomb shelter when Glenn McDole picked him off the ground by his butt and pitched him down the cliff.

Eugene Neilson of South Logan, Utah, who made a mad, bloody dash through the barbed wire at the prison camp and swam under heavy fire away from the beach that day, lives in South Ogden, Utah. When he got out of the service, he went to work for the U.S. Postal Service, did some work on the railway postal service and then later worked at a nearby air base. He raised four children, three girls and a boy. He's in his late 80s now. About 35 years after he left the service, doctors discovered what they thought was a blood clot in his leg. When the surgeon opened him up, he found a calcium-encrusted, .26-caliber Japanese rifle bullet. Apparently, when Nielsen was shot, the bullet took a right turn and went deeper into his leg. That's why the Filipinos couldn't find it when they treated his wound on Palawan.

Fern Barta cannot be located. At last report, he lived in Kingston, Washington, but there is no longer any telephone listing for him.

Ernest Jean Koblos of Chicago, Illinois, could not be located.

Edwin Petry of Santa Monica, California, another escapee, could not be located.

Albert Pacheco of Deming, New Mexico, could not be located. Up until September of 2002, he was listed in the Deming phone directory.

In all probability, some of those that couldn't be located are dead, or because of war or age-induced infirmities, are living in nursing or retirement homes. Some may simply have moved elsewhere in the country.

Donald H. Thomas, Palawan's cobbler who left the island and took one of the infamous hell ships to Japan, where he resumed his work as a slave laborer, returned to Iowa after the war. He went to school on the GI Bill and became a high school art teacher. Thomas and his wife, Jean, live in Winterset, Iowa, where he taught school for 33 years. The couple celebrated their 50th anniversary in 1997, and both are in good health.

15

The Places

Los Baños, the Philippines

Los Baños, where Glenn McDole got his first taste of combat, is a thriving resort area today. It has numerous hotels, all with piped-in thermal spring water, and the city is the site of the University of the Philippines College of Agriculture. It was there that in February of 1945, the Provisional Reconnaissance Platoon of the 11th Airborne Division slipped through enemy lines and paved the way—killing guards and wiping out pillboxes—for an airborne assault which saved the lives of prisoners interned in a Japanese prison camp nearby.

Corregidor

Corregidor, where Mac, his buddies, and thousands of other soldiers, sailors, Marines and Filipino troops surrendered to the Japanese, is a national shrine. There is a Pacific War Memorial on the island, and since the mid–1950s, it has been the site of a military training camp in counter-guerrilla tactics.

Cabanatuan

With a population of well over 200,000, Cabanatuan today is the commercial center for the eastern portion of Luzon's central plain, an area heavily farmed in rice. The rail spur line from Manila ends there. It is the same line that Glenn and his buddies took in those tiny metal boxcars so many years ago. Those weakened by lack of food and wounds from battle died standing in the suffocating heat as the Philippine sun beat down upon the cars. The Cabanatuan American Memorial, erected by the survivors of the Bataan Death March, is located there. It is a beautiful, park-like memorial and is maintained by the American Battle Commission.

Puerto Princesa, Palawan Island

Palawan today is a thriving tourist attraction, thanks to the infusion of Japanese and Filipino money. Puerto Princesa boasts luxurious hotels and sandy beaches. About a half-million people live on Palawan and the other islands within its jurisdiction. It is rich in timber and minerals. For those who like to swim, scuba dive, deep-sea fish, or study the flora and fauna of the island's rain forests and mountains, it is paradise.

Epilogue

When American troops landed on Palawan in early 1945, there wasn't much left of the prison, except for the bomb shelters the prisoners had dug for themselves. Soldiers entering Camp 10A found nothing but the bones of dead Americans scattered throughout the trenches, and it was apparent what had happened. There were charred remains everywhere and clear indicators that dynamite had been used in an attempt to cover up the massacre.

When the war ended, the Catholic church in Puerto Princesa, which had been destroyed by American bombers, was rebuilt by the American military.

One American soldier, wandering through the motor pool, came across a diary of the day-to-day happenings and concerns of the Japanese sergeant major who was in charge of the prisoners who worked in the motor pool. He did not write his name in the diary, and, in all probability he was killed in action when American troops hit the beach. We'll never know who he was. Aside from Smiley, the sergeant major was the only other Japanese guard at Palawan Barracks who showed any humanity toward his prisoners. Here is part of what he wrote:

> Nov. 15, 1944—*At the time I landed at Palawan Island, I disliked the prisoners of war, but now I am getting accustomed to them. They certainly work hard. They are quite adept in mechanical work. They certainly are carefree and it appears that they devote no thoughts to the fact that they are prisoners of war.*

> December 7, 1944—*All day I had idle chatter with the prisoners who seem to be learning a little of the Japanese language.*

December 15, 1944—*Due to the sudden change of situation, the 150 prisoners of war were executed. Those who escaped were discovered this morning in the Puerto Princessa antiaircraft trench and were shot. They truly died a pitiful death. The ones who worked in the repair shop really worked hard. From today on I will not hear the familiar greeting, "Good morning, Sergeant Major." "____" who used to reiterate how he wished this war would end so that he could rejoin his parents, or "___" who entered service after three months of married life and who often used to boast about how much his wife must be missing him. I no longer can greet them in this world.*

December 16, 1944—*According to an intelligence report, the enemy landed on Mindoro. It is a miracle to be safe after such a heavy air attack today. Furthermore, if the enemy had landed yesterday, I wonder what would have happened to me. I could have been like the executed prisoners, floating and rolling in the breakwaters.*

January 9, 1945—*After a long absence, I visited the motor vehicle repair shop. Today, the shop is a lonely place. The prisoners who were assisting us there are now just white bones on the beach washed by the waves. Furthermore, there are numerous corpses in the nearby garage and the smell is unbearable. It gives me the creeps.*

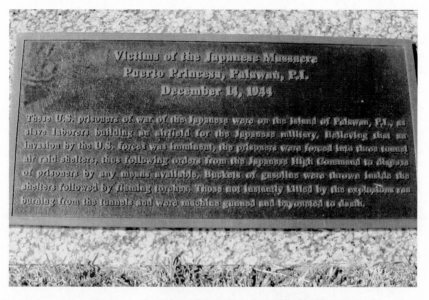

The new Palawan grave marker at Jefferson Barracks in St. Louis. It gives more details of what happened on Palawan (Kathy and Glenda McDole).

There were no more entries in the diary.

The bones of 123 Palawan victims were dug up and returned to the United States, where they were interred on February 14, 1952, in a burial plot at Jefferson Barracks National Cemetery in St. Louis, Missouri. The remains of 16 other Palawan victims could not be located. If you should visit the cemetery, you'll find the Palawan victims in Section 85. It is the largest group burial in the cemetery, all of them at rest with other veterans who served and died in all of America's wars.

On October 4th, 2003, a bright, sunny fall day in St. Louis, about 100 people gathered at Jefferson Barracks National Cemetery to dedicate a new plaque at the site of the grave of the 123 identified victims of the Palawan Massacre. The new plaque gives a better account of what occurred that day. Glenn McDole and Eugene Nielsen were there and told the relatives and friends of the men buried there what had happened that day. Then the list of all of those killed on Palawan was read aloud:

Victims of the Palawan Massacre, December 14, 1944

Jewett Franklin Adams	San Diego, California
Robert Arthur Adkins	Ocean Lake, Oregon
Robert S. Anderson	Harper, Washington
Henry H. Araujo	Denver, Colorado
Heraclio S. Arispe	Corpus Christi, Texas
Arthus Anton Arnoldy	Tipton, Kansas
Homer R. Bailey	Ardmore, Oklahoma
Herbert Baker	Address Unknown
Everett R. Bancroft, Jr.	Canon City, Colorado
Carl Ellis Barnes	Bakersfield, California
Darrell Leroy Barnes	Address Unknown
Charles W. Bartle	Coffeyville, Kansas
Benjamin F. Beason	Canyon, Texas
Wilbur Burdett Blackburn	Wichita, Kansas
Mason J. Bouchey	Saginaw, Michigan
William T. Brown	Antioch, California
Fred T. Bruni	Janesville, Wisconsin
Vernon Edward Buchanon	Turner, Kansas
Douglas Burnett	LeGrande, Oregon
Sammy Lee Caldwell	San Angelo, Texas
Casey Carter	Paris, Texas
Roy R. Childers	New Berlin, Illinois
James L. Choate	Madisonville, Kentucky

Harry Cook	Address Unknown
Earl J. Crandell	Scipio, Oklahoma
William T. Cravens	Port Royal, Kentucky
Franklin A. Cullins	Black Oak, Arkansas
John Czajkowski	Nichols, Wisconsin
John F. Diaz	Osage, Iowa
Glen A. Dutton	Clovis, New Mexico
Clayton E. Elix	Pueblo, Colorado
Erving A. Evans	Huron, South Dakota
George R. Eyre	Marion, Ohio
Houston E. Fletcher	Oklahoma City, Oklahoma
William Ferson Fryar	Apollo, Pennsylvania
Jessie R. Gee	Yuba City, California
Bill Edmond Gillespie	Dallas, Texas
Joseph Charles Glacken, Jr.	St. Louis, Missouri
Sammy Glover	Daisetta, Texas
Richard E. Goodykoontz	Marion, Indiana
James Dewey Grahnert	Vancouver, Washington
Mike P. Giuffreda	San Jose, California
Waldo Stedem Hale	Saybrook, Illinois
William Lester Hammock, Jr.	Dermott, Arkansas
Dane H. Hamric	Widen, West Virginia
Kenneth Russell Hansen	San Luis Obispo, California
Lenton R. Harbin	Shreveport, Louisiana
John Solomon Harris	Monticello, Georgia
Douglas F. Hawkins	Coeburn, West Virginia
Clifford Marlin Henderson	Reed, West Virginia
Joseph P. Henderson	Los Angeles, California
Roy J. Hicks	Crestview, Florida
Miner C. Hinkle	Calexico, California
Robert L. Hubbard	Reno, Nevada
Hugh B. Hubbard	Reno, Nevada
John F. Hughes	Richmond, Virginia
Tom V. Huston	Modesto, California
Fred W. Hutchison	Los Angeles, California
Charles D. Jacobson	Denver, Colorado
Aubrey Peyton Johnson	Winnisbora, Louisiana
Earl E. Joyner	Goshen Springs, Mississippi
Joseph Kazlauskas	Lowell, Massachusetts
Richard Kernes	Address Unknown
Wilfred Kernes	Madrid, Iowa
Harold W. King	Topeka, Kansas

Henry Carlisle Knight	Portland, Oregon
Richard A. Koerner	Little Falls, Minnesota
Steven Thaddeus Kozuch	Chicago, Illinois
Arthur L. Lamountain	Millers Falls, Massachusetts
Leo N. Lamshire, Jr.	Philadelphia, Pennsylvania
Kenneth L. Lewis	Taunton, Massachusetts
Forest E. Lindsay	Vale, North Carolina
Kenneth Clyde Lindsey	Gillette, Wyoming
John A. Lyons	North Staples, Minnesota
Carl Louis Mango	Harrisburg, Pennsylvania
George V. Manzi	Bridgeport, Connecticut
Donald Joseph Martyn	Hollywood, California
Jose E.T. Mascarenas	Penasco, New Mexico
Richard E. McAnany	Conemaugh, Pennsylvania
William M. McElveen	New Orleans, Louisiana
Theodore McNally	Slayton, Texas
Joe. B. Million	Harrodsburg, Kentucky
Fred V. Moffatt	Moline, Illinois
Roger G. Moore	Monroe, Louisiana
E. C. Morris	Jacksboro, Texas
Orland Otis Morris	Warren, Idaho
Levi D. Mullins	Address Unknown
Frank R. Newell	Tonawanda, New York
Harry Noel	Chicago, Illinois
Ernest J. Novak	Watsonville, California
Trinidad F. Otero	Willard, New Mexico
James A. Pitts	Winter Garden, Florida
Dillard Price	Magnolia, Arkansas
Homer F. Rankin	Freeport, Kansas
Daniel Woodrow Ray	Austin, Texas
Vernon W. Rector	Phoenix, Arizona
Arthur W. Rhoades	Fort Wayne, Indiana
Peter Tom Rigas	Chicago, Illinois
James Howard Roe	Chase, Kansas
James R. Rudd	Cutuno, Kentucky
Santiago S. Saiz	Peralta, New Mexico
John Sanchez	Kansas City, Missouri
Henry F. Scally	Silver City, New Mexico
Charles A. Schubert	Albuquerque, New Mexico
Edward Joseph Schultz	Pittsville, Wisconsin
Raymond Lewis Seagraves	Lewisville, Texas
Charles E. Shalley	Address Unknown

Gabriel Sierra, Jr.	Randsburg, California
Jesse Herschel Simpson	Wichita, Kansas
Charlie Sirfus	Des Moines, Iowa
Owen Neil Skaggs	San Francisco, California
William Burleigh Skidmore	Los Angeles, California
Kenneth O. Smith	Hoisington, Kansas
Julio F. Smith	Indianapolis, Indiana
Charles Carlyle Smith	Laurenceburg, Tennessee
Cecil J. Snyder	Address Unknown
Carroll F. Spindler	Edwardsville, Illinois
Devert E. Stanley	Dallas, Texas
John M. Stanley	Lakeview, Texas
Robert L. Stevenson	Muskegon, Michigan
James H. Stidham	Hardshell, Kentucky
Charles H. Street	Santa Cruz, California
Harding E. Stutts	Pinetta, Florida
Leslie I. Seany	Hamilton, Missouri
Homer E. Swinney	Hawk Point, Missouri
Glen E. Teel	Columbus Junction, Iowa
Jolly E. Terry	Cahe, Oklahoma
Delbert R. Thomas	Wellington, Kansas
Glenn C. Turner	San Antonio, Texas
Joseph J. Uballe	Boone, Iowa
Ted E. Vitatoe	Rockwood, Tennessee
George McClelland Waddell	Kansas City, Missouri
Carl M. Walker	Elizabeth City, North Carolina
George Murray Walker	Walterboro, South Carolina
John Otis Warren	DeKalb, Mississippi
Horace Whitecotton	Mesa, Arizona
Maurice Scott Williams, Jr.	Kansas City, Missouri
John Grant Williams	Wichita, Kansas
Willard R. Yeast	Harrodsburg, Kentucky

Sources

Brown, Charles T. *Bars from Bilibid Prison.* San Antonio: Naylor, 1947.

Burlage, George. Unpublished manuscript on the Palawan Massacre. Aubrey, Texas, 1984.

Costello, John. *The Pacific War.* New York: Rawson, Wade, 1981.

History of the Defenders of the Philippines, Guam and Wake Islands, 1941–1945. Paducah, KY: Turner, 1991.

The History Place: World War II in the Pacific, Timeline of Events, 1941–1945. *<http://www.historyplace.com/unitedstates/pacificwar/timeline.htm>*

Japanese war crimes trials testimony taken from U.S. War Department files. "Summary No. 306 Subject: Perpetrators of Infamous Palawan Massacre to be tried." (U.S. vs. Seiichi Terada et al.)

Kelly, Arthur L. "Undercover: Willie Smith's Escape." *World War II Magazine*, July 1990.

Kooi, Muriel Byers, with Donald H. Thomas. "The Wrigley Peace Pact of August 17, 1945." Unpublished essay. Winterset, Iowa.

Manchester, William. *American Caesar: Douglas MacArthur 1880–1964.* New York: Dell, 1979.

McDole, Glenn. Interview. Admiral Nimitz Museum and University of North Texas Oral History Collection, #1317. October 10, 1996.

Morris, Eric. *Corregidor: The American Alamo of World War II.* New York: Cooper Square Press, 2000.

Moskin, J. Robert. *The U.S. Marine Corps Story.* 3rd ed., revised. New York: Little, Brown, 1992.

Index